ENTREPRE

ENTREPRENEUR

How to Start an Online Business

Lucy Tobin

CAPSTONE

This edition first published 2012
© 2012 Lucy Tobin

Registered office
Capstone Publishing Ltd. (A Wiley Company), John Wiley and Sons Ltd, The
Atrium, Southern Gate, Chichester, West Sussex, PO19 8SQ, United Kingdom

For details of our global editorial offices, for customer services and for information
about how to apply for permission to reuse the copyright material in this book
please see our website at www.wiley.com.

Wiley publishes in a variety of print and electronic formats and by print-on-
demand. Some material included with standard print versions of this book may not
be included in e-books or in print-on-demand. If this book refers to media such as a
CD or DVD that is not included in the version you purchased, you may download
this material at http://booksupport.wiley.com. For more information about Wiley
products, visit www.wiley.com.

Library of Congress Cataloging-in-Publication Data is available

A catalogue record for this book is available from the British Library.

ISBN 978-0-857-08288-6 (paperback) ISBN 978-0-857-08301-2 (ebk)
ISBN 978-0-857-08302-9 (ebk) ISBN 978-0-857-08303-6 (ebk)

Set in 11/14 pt Adobe Caslon Pro-Regular by Toppan Best-set Premedia Limited
Printed by TJ International Ltd, Padstow, Cornwall, UK

CONTENTS

ACKNOWLEDGEMENTS

There can't be a more helpful group of business people in Britain than entrepreneurs. This book wouldn't have happened without a huge amount of help from founders of web start-ups, financiers, developers and more. Thank you for breaking up your sunny weekends in Chicago, the frantic final hours of acquisitions and the Heathrow check-in queue to talk to me. The entrepreneurial lifestyle is jam-packed, and I'm grateful to all of those included in this book for giving up time to give out advice. Special thanks to Yael Levey and Rob Cooper for the very latest trends on wireframing and more, and to Twitter contact Leigh Caldwell of Inon for his exhaustive advice on development.

This book is for my parents, for being the best backers anyone could ask for, and for Howard, my husband-to-be and PR-in-chief. Thank you.

ABOUT THE AUTHOR

Lucy Tobin is a business reporter for the *London Evening Standard*, where she writes a column about entrepreneurs and how they built up their companies. She has been named Enterprise and Business Journalist of the Year in the Santander Media Awards Young Journalist of the Year by law firm DLA Piper; commended as Journalist to Watch at the WorkWorld Media Awards and as Regional Journalist of the Year at the HeadlineMoney awards for financial journalism. Lucy is the author of two previous books, *A Guide to Uni Life* and *Pimp Your Vocab*. She has a first class degree in English from Oxford University. www.lucytobin.com

INTRODUCTION

Heard the old joke about the new entrepreneur? A bloke who's just launched an online business meets some friends in the pub. 'So', says one, 'what made you decide to start up on your own?' 'Well', replies the entrepreneur, 'it was something my last boss told me.' His friend responds: 'Wow, what did he say?' – to which our hero responds: 'You're fired.'

Groans all round. Not only because it's a pretty bad joke, but also because it just doesn't represent the vibrant culture of entrepreneurship in the UK today. Yes, it's true that during the recession, hundreds of thousands of Britons realised there was an alternative to spending each night worrying about the corporate axe and whether they'd still have a job in the morning. Amid a culture of no pay-rises and ever-longer hours, many turned away from spending their working life slaving away for someone else, and started up alone.

But for hordes of other entrepreneurs, launching a start-up is no longer a back-up option if all else fails, but an exciting career choice. Lord Sugar, Donald Trump and their Apprentices can take a lot of the credit, so too can the Dragons in their Den. But it's not just that. New graduates, corporate executives and stay-at-home parents are all electing to create their own businesses from scratch and work incredibly hard to turn them into a soaring success precisely because being an entrepreneur is an enormously fulfilling career choice.

Online, the potential is even bigger because becoming an internet entrepreneur is very accessible. Whether you're setting up a shop, inventing a new service, creating a niche talking-spot or connecting up international markets, anyone with a computer, mouse and a bit of nous can do so on the internet more cheaply and easily than doing so on the high street or in bricks and mortar.

That's why for every mega-famous internet entrepreneur like Facebook's Mark Zuckerberg – in his late-20s, worth $16 billion – and Natalie Massenet, who founded luxury fashion retailer Net-a-Porter in 2000 and sold it for £350 million a decade later – there are lesser-known internet start-ups making their creators bountiful revenue streams.

There are people like Hayley Parsons, founder of the GoCompare insurance comparison outfit, and Nick Robertson, a millionaire several times over after floating online clothes retailer Asos. com. There are 'intrepreneurs' who've become famous and powerful through their online creations, like Justine Roberts, co-founder of Mumsnet, whose site is courted by election-nervous politicians.

And then there's the other part of the online business ecosystem: the millions of people making smaller, steady incomes from particular ideas. There's Jonathan Hartland, a City suit who quit his lucrative accountancy job to start up an online Craigslist-style noticeboard, BigBleu.com, designed exclusively for employees of the world's big law firms, banks, and corporates. Or there's Joshua Magidson, who set up eatstudent.co.uk, allowing students to access local takeaway menus and have food delivered straight to their halls of residence, whilst still a fresher at Nottingham University. He recently graduated, and sold it a year after graduating for what he calls a 'really, really good amount' to industry giant justeat.co.uk.

Most entrepreneurs were once, like the rest of us, stuck lemming-like on the commuter conveyor belt, until one day they had a good idea and decided to break free and make it work. So, who are they, how did they do it and – most importantly – what are their secrets so you can do it too? That's what this book is all about.

In my job as a business reporter on the *London Evening Standard* newspaper, I write a column about entrepreneurs. Every week, I meet business founders who tell me about their route from start-up to steady earner. Their ideas are all very different. I've featured a make-up tycoon and a baby-bottle inventor, a music festival creator and a barbecue designer. But, whatever their business, these entrepreneurs all have some characteristics in common. They're all passionate – obsessively so – about their companies. They're all adamant that they could never again work for someone else. They're all excellent networkers.

After a while, I began to notice that many of the entrepreneurs had something else in common: they'd all faced similar problems and made similar mistakes at the start of their businesses. Many regretted waiting till a website was 'perfect' before going live and missing the chance of a head start on the competitors. Many said they'd misunderstood online marketing strategies and hadn't realised until they'd wasted thousands of pounds.

I began to wonder whether wannabe entrepreneurs could learn from the mistakes of existing ones by reading about the biography of a start-up, from conception through development, to launch and beyond. I started pondering the value of an entrepreneur's handbook, with inspiration from the industry's most successful stars. Then, as every entrepreneur I met emitted radiant excitement about the enormous opportunities online and the accessibility of the web, I realised internet start-ups were the area of the future, which any kind of guide should focus on.

So where do the best entrepreneurs get their big ideas? In the bath? On the train? Actually, it's rarely so simple. Most admit inspiration didn't actually whack them over the head, but was squeezed out: after searching for business ideas everywhere, then brainstorming, researching and honing, trying and sometimes failing, eventually they struck gold. Many conjured up their big ideas from annoying or frustrating situations, which they wanted to create a business to fix.

You might be surprised by the development stories behind some of our most popular websites, from charity firm Just-Giving (idea fleshed out during a late-night phone call) and card-maker Moonpig (created after its founder received a job pay-off). You can find out that, and much more, in their founders' stories in the first half of the book. Then see Chapter 12, The Lightbulb Moment, to work on finding your own inspiration.

Time, though, for a reality check. The majority of new businesses fail within their first few years. Even once you've found IT, that Big Idea, your work has only just begun. That will become clear when you read about the early days of the now-very-successful online business card company Moo.com. Founder Richard Moross had originally conceived a business called 'pleasure cards', which people would use to communicate online – a kind of early form of social networking. But when he discovered no one liked his idea, he had to change his site's entire strategy as well as its name and marketing before hitting the right formula with Moo.

There's no disguising the sweat involved in a start-up. It's true that you can't switch on the TV without finding eager candidates on BBC's *Dragons' Den* waxing lyrical about why their business is going to take over the world tomorrow, or wannabes on *The Apprentice* spouting about why they'll be the new Lord Sugar by the end of the week. But know this: it won't happen overnight. To launch a successful online start-up requires market research, budgeting, technological wizardry – your own or borrowed – fundraising, business administration, networking, marketing, analytics and much more. This book will show you how.

Entrepreneur includes a cornucopia of web start-up success stories in sectors ranging from moneylending to birthday cards, lettings to furniture, parental advice to insurance. The business founders reveal all about how they did it, their triumphs and failures, advice and warnings, and their top tips on how you can follow in their footsteps.

The government keeps promising that the country's future growth will be led by a burst of entrepreneurship. As Prime Minister, David Cameron, put it at celebrations for Global Entrepreneurship Week: 'The future of our economy depends on a new generation of entrepreneurs coming up with ideas, resolving to make them a reality and having the vision to create wealth and jobs.' A string of funding and advisory initiatives are now in place to help wannabe entrepreneurs take the leap (find out more on funding in Chapter 14, Setting up a Business, and in the Resources section at the end of this book). A host of dynamic start-up networks are waiting to hear your ideas. A huge pool of British consumers, who are known for lapping up new ideas, are all egging you on.

So, whether you're a bored executive, sick of the hamster wheel of corporate life, a university leaver, fresh out of academia and inspired to go it alone, or an ambitious go-getter, keen to hold down an existing job whilst launching a bright idea: there's never been a more exciting time to be an entrepreneur. Find out here how scores of other entrepreneurs made it, then give it a go yourself. Work hard, enjoy it – and turn yourself into a success entrepreneur.

Part One: The Story Behind . . .

CHAPTER 1

WONGA

Errol Damelin hired a creative branding agency to come up with the perfect name for his new website, the money-lending business that we now know as Wonga. It was the type of agency that the Government hired to create the much-derided Olympic logo. It was expensive. It was, Damelin told me when we met a few weeks shy of Wonga's fourth birthday, a mistake.

'The agency sent through long lists of names with endless analysis about each one', he remembers. 'They did a lot of work – but they had to, to justify their fee. Nothing stood out. Then my co-founder and I were talking to friends about the name over drinks one day, and they suggested Wonga. We put it to the branding people, and they sent back a very detailed, rational response about why it was a terrible name. But we loved it – it was short and recognisable.

'There's so much noise online, from hundreds of thousands of financial sites and businesses. We thought the name Wonga would break through that. So we ignored the experts' advice and went with it.' That, says Damelin, is the entrepreneurial way of doing things: 'you take advice, but are confident in your own decisions.'

It's a strategy that has helped Damelin grow Wonga from an interesting idea – to provide an instant, fully automated lending decision over small, short-term loans online, ensuring that the cash arrived in the successful applicants' bank accounts minutes later – to a business that in 2010 brought in £73 million.

Speed and a willingness to quickly respond to customer demand were crucial, says Damelin, a South African who once worked as an investment banker. He quit the industry after becoming more interested in developing ideas himself, and spent five years building up an online marketplace for the cabling industry before selling it in 2005. Damelin then moved to the US for a year to mull his next big idea.

He thought up 'tons' of other start-up business ideas, before rejecting them all, Damelin reveals. But my request to find out more about them was met with a grin and a shaking head. 'I'm still going to build them one day', he says, ever the serial entrepreneur. But how did Damelin know Wonga was *the one*? 'I talked to friends, family, people I knew from business', he says. 'Of all the ideas I thought of, the idea of instant money, available online 24/7 gained most traction.' The lending industry, he thought, 'was well overdue some disruption.'

The idea

'It was clear that there was already a market for short-term cash', Damelin says, sitting near Wonga's Georgian townhouse headquarters, close to Regents Park. 'People were borrowing from friends, using bank overdrafts or payday loans, or going to doorstop lenders and pawnbrokers. But the question for me was, could we use new technology to do it better? Could we automate money-lending, one of the world's oldest industries? And could we use technology to do it with more speed and convenience, and build a trustworthy platform and brand?' The entrepreneur spent 2006 working that out.

He went back to basics. 'I think most people tend to be too incremental, changing too little, when starting a business', he says. 'To create a financial services company, they'd say, "how does Barclays do it? Oh, they've got this application form and this process. Let's do the same, but make our application form green, not red."' Damelin thought everything that existed was 'too slow, too reliant on a man in a suit looking at someone's spending and deciding, sometimes quite arbitrarily, whether to lend to them.'

Creating a series of workflows, he broke his idea down into steps. 'It began with "how do companies make a decision about whether to lend money?"' Damelin explains. 'When someone applied, you would have to make a decision using data, so then I thought, "what data do I need, and where can I get it from?" and went from there.' The entrepreneur arranged meetings with industry experts to learn about the existing technology and retail banking, 'asking a lot of questions and being generally relentless', he says.

Concept to reality

The scale and technical know-how required for the lending website led Damelin to seek out a partner. 'It was too ambitious for me alone', he says. 'For a lifestyle business or a copycat idea, one founder is fine – often the economics won't justify two salaries – but if you want to create a disruptive business – one that changes the industry – you need a partner.'

So Damelin linked up with Jonty Hurwitz, an engineer who had been running a business in the same building as his own a few years earlier. 'Having shared office space with Jonty meant we knew each other well – and trust is important', he explains. 'You want a co-founder who brings something different to the table than you do – whether it's experience, skill, knowledge or even attitude. We spent months prodding the idea, and worked on the brand too – we knew it had to be totally transparent, with no banking jargon. It had to contrast with the big banks, who are totally opaque about how they make their lending decisions and make their money.'

At Wonga, Damelin focused on the commercial side, whilst Hurwitz became chief technology officer. The company put together a board including angel investor Robin Klein, of The Accelerator Group, backer of sites including Graze.com and Tweetdeck, who became Wonga's chairman. Damelin and Hurwitz built a small developer team recruited from their network of techies. Work took place at a serviced office in north London. 'Many start-ups begin at home, but I wanted everyone to be in the same place, sharing learning all the time, and pushing in the same direction', says Damelin.

Wonga developed proprietary technology – it owns thousands of pieces of intellectual property – to check up to 7,500 pieces of information on an applicant before approving a loan. Complex algorithms crunched the data, and the site could then action funds to be transferred into users' bank accounts within 15 minutes. The backend was hugely complex, but the frontend was simple. Wonga developed sliders asking 'how much cash do you want' and 'how long do you want if for'. Applicants could move around the sliding bars, allowing them to see that, for example, borrowing £265 for six days would cost £21.51 in interest and fees. The test site took nine months to build.

Take off

A beta version of Wonga went live in October 2007. 'It was a very soft launch, we simply bought a few Google Adwords to test demand. We didn't want too much volume', says Damelin. 'We had budgeted to do 17 loans in that first month, as we didn't want to get overloaded. But in fact we had four accepted applications on the first day.' The founding team watched over the site like anxious new parents. 'We half expected the system to fall over, though actually it was more robust than we thought.'

The first platform lasted nine months, but after six, the tech team began rebuilding Wonga, creating a second version that was better at sorting data and analysing creditworthiness. It went live in July 2008, and in the 11 months after the revamp, Wonga made 100,000 loans. Revenues in its first 12 months hit £15 million, and the site turned a profit from year one.

Between then and now, little has visually changed on Wonga's homepage – the sliders are still there, the colour scheme is still blue and green. 'Don't obsess over image unless it's critical to the sector you're trying to disrupt', is Damelin's advice.

Wonga's wonga

Money, says Damelin, was never a big problem for Wonga. 'We've always had more demand for funding than we've wanted to take up. We were lucky, I suppose, but mainly it's because the idea was good and the team was backable.' Damelin raised £3 million before starting to build the site. 'A pretty big seed round, but the business was always going to be capital intensive – we needed cash to pay out the loans as well as operate.' The money came from the venture capital fund Balderton Capital, one of the backers of Lovefilm, where Damelin knew a partner well through networking.

Wonga has since raised a total of £93 million in two further fundraising rounds. Its shareholder register includes Meritech Capital Partners, one of Facebook's backers, Accel Partners and Greylock Partners, the original investors in networking site LinkedIn, and five other VCs. 'Since we fund our own balance sheet, and have to pay out the loans, we didn't want to rely on one source of money', says Damelin.

He warns other wannabe start-ups not to expect too much hands-on help from the VC world. 'Too often people take venture capital money and expect the team there to help them with the details of their business. But VCs can't help find sites or hire staff or make a great product –they're sitting on multiple boards, and that's not their job. There are exceptions, but mostly it's about making introductions or providing access to their network of businesses.'

Making a splash

After interviewing Damelin, I bumped into a friend and told him where I'd been. He instantly screwed up his face: 'That bloody annoying advert!' he exclaimed, before launching into a sing-song of its radio theme tune 'Wonga, Wonga, Wonga . . .' Clearly, the ad did its job. TV and radio advertising was one way that the site made its name. Later, Wonga also paid for free New Year's Eve travel on the London Underground ('previous years had seen NatWest be a sponsor – it was a sign of the new order', says Damelin) and sponsored Blackpool football club in its first season in the Premier League.

Wonga's marketing budget is significant, but Damelin says start-ups on a shoestring budget can still get themselves known. 'The rules of supply and demand dictate that the way established firms are currently marketing will already be expensive', he says. 'As an entrepreneur, you have to be non-traditional. Facing bigger players with bigger budgets, the odds are stacked against you. Identify the people you want to be customers, and go and get them, whether via guerrilla marketing, creating controversy, or making a story. The instinct to do what other companies in the same space are doing is probably the wrong thing to do.'

Wonga was very brand-conscious from the start, hiring a communications director two years before a head of sales, in part because the founders were aware that the site was trading in controversial territory. Financial regulation guidelines demand lenders advertise an annual interest charge and, as a short-term lender, Wonga's APR can be up to 4000%. But Damelin hits back that APR is a 'misleading' comparison for very short-term credit: Wonga's maximum lending period is 30 days, and the interest isn't compounded. Still, Wonga's detractors call it a 'legal loan shark'.

'We realised from the start there was going to be controversy', says Damelin. 'But we had confidence in what we were doing and have always been very keen to talk to anyone who is interested. We were very proactive, going out to do roadshows, speaking to consumer groups, financial regulators, journalists. We wanted to show people why we were different before they jumped to conclusions.'

Today Wonga has provided more than 3.5 million loans, and its revenue soared by 300% between 2009 and 2010. City rumours swirl about a future stock exchange listing and expansion into overseas markets, but Damelin says he's 'not thinking about an exit'.

'I walk into the Wonga office every day and I feel amazingly proud of it', he says. 'A few years ago, it was a pure concept. We made it into something real. There are hundreds of thousands of customers, and people wearing Wonga shirts, Wonga ads on TV and radio, Wonga-sponsored teams at football matches. Something exists that wasn't there before. When you start a business online and get it right, it can be very financially rewarding. But really, it's far more than that.'

Fact box: Wonga

Launch: 2007

Revenues: £73m in 2010

Staff: Over 200

Top tip: 'Be honest with yourself about what you want out of life, how big your idea really is, and the associated effort and personal investment required. That way, you'll stand a far greater chance of succeeding.'

Chapter 2

MOONPIG

If Nick Jenkins had put all his efforts into his first business idea, rather than his third, Britain would have a far wider choice of exotic mushrooms. If he'd gone for his second, thousands more Japanese salarymen might today be speaking perfect English. But Jenkins went for his third, a website selling personalised greetings cards. And as a result, three million people last year opened an envelope to discover their face on the front of *Oi!* magazine or one of Moonpig's thousands of other cards.

The idea was planted in the late 1990s: Jenkins had just quit his first job after university, working as a commodities trader for metals firm Glencore in Moscow. A brush with a shady Russian businessman had led to a death threat nailed to the door of his flat. The Englishman fled back home, cashed in his Glencore shares and decided, 'I wanted to do my own thing, although I wasn't sure what.' Jenkins enrolled on a year-long MBA at Cranfield University, and spent all his time 'thinking up cunning business plans'. The first was the exotic mushrooms. 'Not that kind', he adds. 'Russians love picking and eating mushrooms of every variety, but all we had in England at the time was the dull button variety. So I thought about starting a company selling them to retailers.'

But wary of the way supermarkets squeeze suppliers, he dumped that idea and moved onto the next: teaching English to Japanese businessmen via VoIP technology, like Skype. 'I worked out I could have teams of San Franciscans – because they're on the same time zone – teaching Mr Fukiyama for an hour at a time, then moving on to his colleague. But this was a while before broadband was widespread, and the technology wasn't good enough.'

Jenkins examined several monetisation plans for internet start-ups. 'I looked at the various ways to make money online. With a site funded by advertising I thought you'd need to attract visitors with good content, which would be expensive, and a tough model to crack. Then I thought about selling something physical. But I realised that you'd have to undercut the High Street, and someone could easily come along and undercut you.' So the entrepreneur decided instead to use the internet to sell goods that were different from those on offer on the High Street. He had always sent friends birthday cards with the generic messages Tippexed out and replaced with his own, and decided personalised greeting cards were his ticket to success. 'They have', he adds, 'great margins. The most valuable thing you can print on paper, apart from money. And they are very easy to post.'

Green light

After fleshing out the idea, Jenkins decided to use some of the proceeds of his Glencore share sale – £160,000 – to set up an online greeting cards business. Later, once the website was live, several angel investors invested a further £500,000. 'At the start, I wanted large scale VC backing but with hindsight we got a better result by staying lean', he explains. 'Angel investors are definitely the best way forward. VCs aren't really interested in most start-ups. They came offering me funding once Moonpig was established, but they always do that: offer money when you don't need it.'

The website's name came from an unusual source. 'I wanted something no more than two syllables long, phonetic, catchy, visual and available', the entrepreneur explains. He spent three days trying to find names like 'RedDog' or 'bluepig' but discovered everything had been secured on the web already. Moonpig eventually came to mind as it was one of his nicknames at school. 'I didn't dream I'd still be using the word today', Jenkins admits.

Moving into an office space in Chelsea at the start of 2000, he found a publisher who agreed to license card designs to Moonpig in exchange for a small equity stake. Jenkins outsourced the site's development to an agency ('with little thought how – they may have been just the first one I found') to build the backend of the site. Software linked up personalised orders – with customers able to upload photos, write messages in sand on images of beaches or etch wishes on pictures of wedding rings – with printers. Production was all to take place in-house, since printing had to take place to order. Kenkins reasoned that dong so, whilst expensive, at least meant no wasted stock and easier cash flow.

Yet the launch of Moonpig went about as smoothly as sandpaper. At the time, the site had a team of ten – Jenkins, plus card designers, IT experts, a printer and a duo of marketing specialists. Moonpig was ready to launch in April 2000 and the team planned a party, taking over an e-bar in Fulham with 40 computer screens, and inviting friends, investors and the media so 'people could eat, drink and play with the site.' But that didn't happen: the bar's internet was down for two hours, a huge traffic jam nearby meant none of the journalists turned up, and

Moonpig's database broke down shortly after the party, losing all the orders and not doing much for the site's reputation. The site effectively collapsed just before it went live.

'The website hadn't been built properly, it was all a bit amateur', Jenkins admits. 'So I decided to hire a developer in-house. It meant things got done on time, rather than with an agency where they can take ages in order to bill you more, or because they've got other things going on.'

On the up

Happily for Jenkins, Moonpig survived but, at times, he wasn't sure it would. 'It was painful at first. We had sales of £2000 a month at the start, and it only built up slowly. The first year's turnover hit £90,000. But that still meant we made a £1 million loss. Not even my mum bought a card during that first year – or in fact the four following ones: she couldn't figure out the technology. And then there was the dotcom crash.

'There were moments of despair. I worried it would never work. The site was popular amongst its users, but was growing far too slowly to reach profitability before we ran out of money, and I couldn't think of any ways to spend money to make it grow faster.' Eventually, Jenkins decided to take the opposite track, cutting back overheads by making some of his staff redundant and axing all marketing to allow organic growth to take its course.

It's crucial, he now advises wannabe entrepreneurs, to focus on organic growth. 'If you know that, without spending a penny on marketing, your business will still grow, then you'll be OK', he says. Moonpig's revenues did indeed grow steadily, reaching a turnover of £300,000 in the site's second year, and £500,000 in the third. The first year's £1 million loss slimmed to £700,000 in the second year, then £500,000 in the third, and £300,000 in the fourth, before Moonpig broke even five years after its birth. That was the first year Jenkins took a salary out of the business – 'there was no point beforehand, as I was still putting my own money in' – but he had always expensed a £50,000 salary every year, noting it in the company accounts as a liability to him payable when the company made a profit, and he says other entrepreneurs should do the same.

'You need to place a value on your own time', he says. 'Founders should always take a notional salary, and put it down as a liability in the annual accounts. Then, when the company moves into profit, nobody can question your right to take your unpaid salary, particularly new investors who didn't witness the earlier sacrifices you made.'

Spiralling success

By the time it turned a first profit in 2005, Moonpig's customer numbers had ballooned above three million. It was sending out some 25,000 cards – most costing £2.99 – every day, and had found another revenue stream by signing a tie-up with a florist. Recipients of Moonpig cards were reported to include Tony Blair and the Queen. Their cards might have come from one of over 10,000 Moonpig designs, from cards inviting senders to upload a photo to be a cover model on the latest edition of *Vague* or *Jugs* magazines, to those wishing recipients congratulations on passing a driving test – with fluffy, personalised dice hanging from the wing mirror.

Many of the designs easily transferred to English-speaking customers abroad, says Jenkins of his decision to expand Moonpig overseas around the time it started to make a profit in the UK, first in Australia in 2004, then the US in 2008. At one point, Jenkins paid a branding agency £20,000 to review Moonpig's logo and design. 'All they did was recommend the pig logo had some eyebrows!' he laughs. But most of the site's growth, Jenkins maintains, was always through recommendation.

Jenkins puts much of Moonpig's success down to its staff, and the culture he fostered in the workplace. He sponsored two micropigs – Steph and Kew – for the company and they made monthly visits to Chelsea headquarters from their Kew Gardens home. 'That was great but it's not those kinds of ideas that really make the difference', he says. 'Businesses fail because they skimp on staff, they use interns who come and go so the company can't build up the knowledge and expertise it needs. I tried to create a great constructive working environment where staff knew that good work and talent was rewarded, and nobody got shouted at for making an honest mistake. If you look after people and give them opportunities to grow, they'll stick with you.'

Funding

Jenkins gradually raised £2.4 million for Moonpig, diluting his own stake in the process. His biggest backers were on his board. 'Never have an advisor on board who's not an investor', the entrepreneur warns. 'If they've stuck their own money into the company, they'll be there at every board meeting with advice and ideas. If not, well, why would they bother?'

With more investment, Jenkins was forced to think about Moonpig's structure. 'It's very hard to take money from investors and not have some kind of exit in mind', he says. 'And with 90% of my assets tied up with the business, there was no way I was going to hand it over to someone else to run.' Jenkins had received 'lots' of bid approaches whilst running the company and, in 2010, began talking to some of them. 'I wanted a company who would add value to the business, not just offer a big cheque', he says. In July 2011, the entrepreneur sold Moonpig to online digital photo business PhotoBox in a deal worth £120 million. Jenkins pocketed a windfall worth some £42 million, retaining a 5% stake in the new company.

'PhotoBox was the best option for a sale', he says. 'Moonpig will benefit from its expertise – more manufacturing capacity, a big presence in continental Europe – and piggy back on its sales.' There are, says Jenkins, 'quite a few Moonpig millionaires', – not just him but staff as well as investors. The entrepreneur, however, still isn't sure what he'll do with his enormous cheque. 'I had lots of ideas about what I'd do with the money if I sold the company but I have realised that most material things are more exciting when they are still unaffordable. The real value of money is the freedom it gives', he says. 'You shouldn't build a business just to sell it. Building a business is a really enjoyable process, and the difficult times make the success even more satisfying.'

Fact box: Moonpig

Launch: 2000

Revenues: £31 million in year to April, 2011. Pre-tax profit of £11.2 million

Staff: 100

Top tip: 'Be convinced your product is something that people actually want. Sounds simple, but if it is, customers will do your marketing for you, and that's half the work done.'

CHAPTER 3

MUMSNET

When Justine Roberts took her one-year-old twins on holiday to Florida in 1999, the family-friendly resort promised in the travel brochure didn't quite match the reality. 'It was a disaster', Roberts remembers. 'It was our first holiday abroad with the kids, and we hadn't thought through the time differences or journey. The kids spent the whole plane journey vomiting, and when we arrived they woke up at 2 a.m. every day. There were supposed to be childcare facilities in the hotel, but the staff didn't have any training or interest in children. So all of the parents were sitting around the pool bemoaning our choice.'

Roberts, however, didn't just moan about it: she took action. 'At the time, everyone was having an internet idea, and I started thinking, wouldn't it have been nice if there had been a place to swap info about this rubbish hotel before we'd forked out all this cash and time trying to get the twins abroad?' She thought the internet would be 'a good vehicle for pooling info with other parents, who'd been there and done that.' There was, Roberts maintains, 'no brilliance, just the idea of letting people tap into others' ideas.'

Just over a decade on, and that simple idea has morphed into Mumsnet, a parenting forum with 35 million page views every month and 25,000 posts a day. It has developed such a reputation in the corridors of Westminster and in the boardrooms of retailers that newspapers have described Roberts as one of the most powerful women in Britain. The holiday-inspired website has grown into a campaigning voice and a force feted by manufacturers for product recommendations.

Jacuzzi business

But, at the start, Roberts thought her online idea would be a part-time extra to be fitted in alongside trips to the gym. 'I'd been casting around for something to do since becoming a parent', she explains. 'After having children I didn't want to go back to traditional work – I'd been a sports reporter, dashing around the country all the time. So this kind of project seemed ideal.' After flying in from Florida, Roberts asked a friend with a technical background to build the Mumsnet website in return for a chunk of the future company.

She then asked Carrie Longton, a TV producer whom she knew from antenatal classes, to be a co-founder of the site. 'I wanted a partner because I didn't want to work every hour of the day', explains Roberts. 'Of course, that's exactly what I did end up doing. Still, back then I convinced Carrie we'd have this wonderful work–life balance and work meetings in the jacuzzi at our local gym. We did try it once, but the paper got soggy.'

Longton didn't even have a computer, and had to rush out to buy one. Just how little the web had taken off back then – only 12 years ago – was evidenced by Roberts' attempt to buy business cards. 'It was the dotcom boom, everyone was raising millions so we thought we'd better organise a business plan and raise money like the rest of them', she explains. 'We worked out a revenue plan – on-site adverts and e-commerce – and started to approach contacts, VCs, people who we knew had money, any leads we could. On the way to an event at First Tuesday [a technology networking group] to meet potential investors, I went to a printer in King's Cross to order some business cards. But they didn't have an "@" sign for an email address. That was a bit of a sign of the times.'

Dodgy business cards weren't the only reason Mumsnet failed to raise any significant early backing. 'Just as we were punting our idea around, Boo.com failed, and the whole funding market collapsed.' Instead Roberts organised a £20,000 loan from a friend to cover early costs and commission content for their site, but resigned themselves that its growth was going to have to be organic – and slow. 'A back-bedroom affair', as Roberts puts it, 'which actually suited us – with our young kids – much better. The responsibility of hiring hundreds of people and renting a huge office in Clerkenwell wouldn't have worked. In hindsight, not managing to raise any money was probably a good thing.'

Word of mouth

The website went live, and grew slowly. 'At the start', Roberts admits, 'the forums were full of my own posts – I had more than one user name and kept asking questions and then answering them myself.' Early on in the life of Mumsnet, the team spent £100 promoting their site in an advert in listing magazine *Time Out Kids*. 'But traditional marketing wasn't for us', says Roberts. 'We didn't have the budget, and had to be more imaginative. So we pleaded with members to talk about us and recommend friends, and sent them posters to put up at local nurseries.' Roberts' experience working as a journalist helped too. 'I wrote a big piece on a diary of a dotcom start-up for *The*

Times' Saturday Magazine, which brought in a lot of people. I continuously tried to think of ideas that editors might like to boost user numbers. What helped enormously too was the fact that the site was free.'

Mumsnet's most popular discussion topic was then, as it remains now, 'am I being unreasonable . . .', covering everything from mother-in-laws to toddler tantrums. But, whilst the forum was gradually growing in popularity, its metrics were going in the opposite direction. 'Thanks to the dotcom crash, the advertising market collapsed in our first six months after going live', says Roberts. 'Ad revenues fell from £25 per page impression to £2.50. The site felt more like an interesting hobby than a business.' What kept the founding team going was fact that parents were beginning to find Mumsnet a helpful resource.

'We started getting e-mails saying, "I was so miserable and alone, Mumsnet saved my life,"' Roberts explains. 'Then one day a pregnant friend phoned and said "I'm having palpitations, did you have them, can you tell me about it?" I said yes, but told her I'd only answer properly if she posted the question online. She agreed, but I felt really guilty about it and rushed to answer her question on the site – but by the time I'd got there, someone else had already replied.

'So whilst Mumsnet wasn't going very well as a business idea, it felt worthwhile and we hoped that, one day, some of that utility would turn into something. It was working as a website long before it was as a business. Mumsnet needed a lot of faith.' For the first five years, that faith also involved a financial hit. 'We didn't pay ourselves a proper salary for the first five years, which meant we couldn't really justify proper childcare', says Roberts. 'I was at home with young twins, and would spend a few hours answering emails and site queries and writing newsletters, with regular interruptions to feed the children or do the laundry. When we wanted to add product reviews to the site, we'd put the kids in their buggies and go to Islington to find parents to fill in our form about buggies. It was very labour intensive, but helped drive traffic.'

How to get known? Get sued

As more users logged into Mumsnet, the press began to turn to Roberts as a voice for mothers, which helped to get the site's name known the site's name around. But Roberts believes the first big story to catapult Mumsnet from niche audience to the mainstream was when Gina Ford, strict parenting guru and author of *The Contented Little Baby Book*, sued the website for libel after Mumsnet users posted allegedly defamatory comments about her. 'I was heavily pregnant with my third child when the lawyers' letters started arriving. It was terribly stressful', says Roberts. The case was eventually settled for a five-figure sum. 'If I'd had more time and resources I'd have taken the case to court. At the time, it was awful, but retrospectively the case was really good for Mumsnet's profile.'

Another path to fame for Mumsnet came in October 2009, when users asked Prime Minister Gordon Brown, a guest on the site's live webchat, to identify his favourite biscuit. Despite being asked 12 times, and Mumsnetters' prompts suggesting that it might be Garibaldi or Nice, the then-prime minister famously refused to divulge. Biscuitgate – and Mumsnet – became a national talking point.

Still flying solo

Twelve years after its creation, Mumsnet has, unusually, never organised any formal rounds of investment beyond its initial

£20,000 start-up fund. Having no shareholders means, says Roberts, 'that we can focus on what's good for the company and the community without investors worrying about us hitting profit targets.' The site has turned down advertising from brands it doesn't approve of, including Nestlé and McDonald's. Roberts adds: 'Overall, we have a very simple way of running the business – we never pay out more than we're getting in. We only hire incrementally, when we can afford people, and not just for a few months but for the next year at least. I have never wanted to expand and then contract because of all the trauma involved.'

Nowadays Mumsnet makes its money through display advertising plus insight market research for parenting product companies. 'Advertisers took a long time to switch from traditional media to new media', says Roberts. 'For our first few years, they were still ploughing money into baby magazines that had a tenth of our circulation, thanks to a general mistrust of forums – odd given advertisers can see our actual user stats. But that's changed now, which should make it easier for new start-ups.'

No exit

Mumsnet's growth plans remain incremental, including expanding Gransnet, a spin-off site for grandparents, launched in May 2011, and pushing Mumsnet's bloggers network, which splits its advertising revenues with blog-writers. The site is also working on new apps and product recommendations. 'We're harnessing the power of Mumsnet in all sorts of ways', Roberts adds, 'whether it's changing government policy or business's views on mums at work or telling people more about items they can buy.' Or, indeed, where to book a child-friendly holiday – I hear Florida is a good destination for those with year-old twins looking for an online business idea.

Roberts admits she's received 'a few approaches' from parties interesting in buying Mumsnet over the years, but says she remains happy at the helm. 'Mumsnet has always been more than a business', she says. 'It's nice to work somewhere where you can set the ethics and the rules. It's a very special community. If we did ever sell, it would have to be a pretty special kind of acquirer.'

Fact box: Mumsnet

Launch: January 2000

Revenues for 2011: over £3 million

Staff: 48

Top tip: 'Listen to your customers, audience or consumers – in our case, they really have come up with most of our best ideas.'

CHAPTER 4

JUSTGIVING

Every month, 42,000 marathon runners, cyclists, abseilers, firewalkers and more create a new charity fundraising page on JustGiving. The website has grown to be used by 15 million people, who have raised over £1 billion for good causes. But Zarine Kharas, one of the brains behind the business, admits that before launch, 'what I knew about charities or small businesses you could write on the back of a very small envelope.'

There was no eureka moment around the creation of JustGiving. 'It started with a phone call very late at night', explains Kharas, who grew up in Pakistan before moving to the UK to study law at Cambridge, then working her way up the ranks in the legal world before moving to investment bank Credit Suisse. 'A former colleague who had started an internet incubator suggested we look at something in the charity space.' This was 2000, the internet was booming and Kharas had an idea. 'I knew very little about early-stage online businesses, but was fascinated by the growing importance of the internet. In that quick phone call, what occurred to me was that fundraising for charities was what the internet was made for. It involved communications, engagement and financial transactions. The internet, I thought, could combine mass communicating and fundraising.'

With most charities back then not involved in the internet – they didn't have the funds to access new technologies – Kharas decided to create a portal for charities to shout about themselves and allow users to donate to them directly. 'I realised even many large charities didn't have an online presence', she says. 'Being an entrepreneur, you don't necessarily need a single brilliant idea – you just need to spot an opportunity.'

Knocking on doors

Kharas quit her job and devoted herself to creating JustGiving. 'The first steps were to secure investment for the site, and bring charities on board.' She thought the latter, at least, would be easy but those in the industry kept telling Kharas the same thing: it'll never work. So, too, did the venture capital funds she approached. 'I had a great advantage with my financial and legal background – it was good preparation for launching a business, from writing a business plan to understanding the financials, but trying to raise capital was still tough', says Kharas, who is now 60. 'I had disheartening meeting after meeting all saying the same thing: "You cannot be serious." That's when they were too polite to laugh.'

The entrepreneur looked at other options, including making JustGiving a charity. 'But it became clear very quickly that philanthropists and foundations were – rightly – far more interested in investing directly into causes, not a technological tool such as ours. We also realised that it would be extremely difficult, if not impossible, for an organisation running on a purely charitable business model to pool the skills and resources required to create and maintain a world-class high-technology service.'

After months of meetings, perseverance eventually paid off: entrepreneur Béla Hatvany, who sold his Silverplatter data business in the US in 2001, agreed to inject £5 million into JustGiving; a third in loans, the rest in equity. 'My advice would be to use all your professional contacts – spread your net as wide as you possibly can to look for backers', says Kharas, 'Don't be afraid to pick up the phone.'

With investment secured, Kharas arranged meetings with hundreds of charities to learn about what they might want from the site. One was Médecins Sans Frontières UK, headed by Anne-Marie Huby, a multi-lingual former journalist and founder of MSF in the UK. 'She walked in, saying "It's all bollocks, you know," Kharas remembers. 'I realised within minutes that she was someone I needed to get on board. Brutally honest feedback is what all start-ups need. You need to bring people on board who complement your strengths – who share your vision, but aren't afraid to criticise.' Huby liked the idea behind JustGiving and quit her job. With Kharas's business background, and Huby's marketing knowledge, the duo set up a small office in Soho.

At the start, JustGiving outsourced its commerce platform to a technology firm called Quantiv. 'In the long run, however, I think it's really important to bring people in-house – that's what we did – as you need to work more closely with the people doing your development, and ensure they have a clear line of sight to your customers', Kharas explains. 'It's especially important if technology is core to your business model. My best piece of advice on keeping costs low is to stay vigilant and always ask – will this bring in revenue and will it ultimately be profitable? It's easy to convince yourself that something is a good idea, but you always have to bring it back to the bottom line – and how soon you can bring it to market. Agility and speed are more important than efficiency in a start-up.'

A runaway success

At its launch, JustGiving was just an online portal for charities, but soon the team thought up the idea of an online sponsorship form, or personalised fundraising page. In 2001, having spent a year securing taxman approval from its Gift Aid-reclamation service, JustGiving's first fundraiser used the site for his London Marathon run. His initial target was £1500, but he ultimately raised £15,000 through his JustGiving page. The idea seemed to work.

'The real tipping point was when we convinced the London Marathon to use JustGiving as its fundraising platform in 2003', says Kharas. 'Things really snowballed from there.' The site cut the amount of time charities had to wait for their cash from months – with paper sponsorship forms, cash and cheques – to a few days through online donations. Charities quickly signed up.

At first, JustGiving didn't charge a monthly subscription fee to charities, 'as we looked to get people on board and prove the value of our service', says Kharas. 'But ultimately we knew that in order to raise the revenue to keep innovating and leading the market, we needed to charge both subscription and transaction fees for the service.' Now the site charges charities a £15 monthly fee plus 5% of each donation.

It took the site five years to break even ('which required even more perseverance from our investors than us') despite having a team of just eight people for the first couple of years. But as JustGiving's online sponsorship forms took off, so did revenues. In 2003 it launched sister site FirstGiving in the US. By 2007, operating profits were £1.5 million on a £5 million turnover. A year later, that grew to £2.2 million on revenues of £7.3 million.

The usefulness of usability

Yet, Kharas says, JustGiving never promoted itself, instead focusing on building a product that was good enough to go viral. 'Our fundraisers and their sponsors, who tell others about their donations through social networking sites, have done all the marketing footwork', she says. The entrepreneur believed the site's growth accelerated because it focused on usability before other e-commerce sites did so. 'In mid-2004, when we redesigned the page-building process to give our fundraisers more freedom, the site grew exponentially', she says. 'Good user experience is the most important element of marketing. It is very hard to achieve because truly listening to users and seeing them rip to shreds the features the team has slaved over for weeks is not good for one's ego. But if you really put the user at the heart of your product development you are more likely to make your site a must-have tool for your users.'

Without a VC looking over the site's shoulder, JustGiving has experimented 'not just with what we do but how we do it', as Kharas puts it. So instead of individual performance-based bonuses, all staff share a proportion of the site's profits, and there's a flexible approach to working practices (whilst taking into account statutory rights). 'We've more or less thrown away the rule book, and simply trust everyone to do the right thing', says Kharas. 'Everyone is a co-owner of the business and is expected to act as such. We have a flat structure without much hierarchy, we have no hard and fast rules on how much holiday staff can take. We don't even have rules on expenses. An innovative organisation does not need people who ask themselves whether they are following procedures, it needs people who are constantly looking for better ways of doing things, and constantly challenging what's been done before.

'We believe it brings out the best in people and therefore works better for the company. The role of management is to provide a compelling vision, and relentlessly ask challenging questions. Working in this way requires people who are totally self-motivated, true team players with their ego in check and able to deal with a lot of ambiguity. Along with skills and expertise, those are the qualities we look for in new hires.'

Keen to stay nimble despite a staff of more than 60, from developers and designers to social media staff and Gift Aid specialists, JustGiving has divided its employees into multi-disciplinary teams, each focused on a particular set of customers, such as fundraisers, donors, small charities and large charities. 'It enables people to live in a quasi-start-up environment, where delighting clients and delivering value fast and frequently are the top priorities', says Kharas. The business has a strong team focus. Indeed, although I interviewed Kharas alone for this book, she emphasises Huby's work throughout and adds: 'One of my key beliefs is that you cannot succeed in building such an enterprise on your own. It requires true team work and complementary strengths.'

Fee storm

The website has, however, faced a backlash from critics who complain that its 5% fees are too high and dock money from charities. Kharas says that shocked her. 'I never expected people to be cynical about an enterprise which is profitable and has a social benefit', she says. 'The fact is that private capital demands proper returns, which means profits, a fair proportion of which may, in the long term, be distributed to investors.' The site tries to overcome criticism with transparency. 'From the beginning, we've been totally open about our fees. We realise that it can be hard for some people to accept that charities do pay for services, from utilities to direct mail – it is an emotional subject.'

JustGiving's growth plans now focus on users accessing the site via mobiles, as well as offering services for companies: it's launching a corporate platform targeted at FTSE 100 firms, which will allow them to use its fundraising software on their own branded websites. The company is also considering setting up in the Far East. But there's still serious potential in the UK: online giving only represents 5% of the fundraising industry.

Kharas' top tips to other start-ups revolve around being flexible and adaptable about goals. 'At some time in the future, your company will be challenged in a way that has no precedent – so be prepared', she says. 'Ask yourself continually, how do I build an organisation that is as nimble as change itself? You also need to leave your ego at the door. I can't remember who it was who said "it's amazing what you can get done if you don't care who gets the credit for it," but it's so true. Listening to your customers, team members, and outside perspectives requires humility. As you grow your management team, which you will eventually do if your early-stage venture gains traction, seek people with humility.'

Lastly, Kharas advises 'you also need courage, perseverance and boldness to pursue your vision in the face of people constantly telling you that something or the other won't work.' One of JustGiving's meeting rooms is called 'Just do it!' Kharas adds: 'Boldness and humility are a difficult balancing act. But entrepreneurship is a profession, with a skill set that can be imparted and learnt. It requires nerves of steel.'

Fact box: JustGiving

Launch: 2001

Revenues: £10.2 million in 2010

Staff: 63

Top tip: 'Focus, focus, focus on whatever your key metric is, whether revenue, traffic, or something else. Do not take ages to bring to market a perfect product. Instead, create a minimal version of an initial product that meets at least some of your customers' key needs, launch early, and iterate frequently. The earlier you find out what works and what does not, the better.'

CHAPTER 5

ZOOPLA

P roperty porn has a nation entranced. It started with Kirsty, Phil and the stream of TV homes shows, then exploded onto the internet, where thousands of nosy neighbours still spend hours salivating over the price Wayne and Sally paid for 38B. But if there was one site that lifted Britons' obsession with property values into a new league of mania, Zoopla was surely it. When the online start-up launched in 2008, it offered visitors the chance to move beyond browsing previous sale prices to estimate current values for their homes. Zoopla was instantly popular and now has some ten million visitors a month. Yet the man behind the site, 37-year-old Alex Chesterman, had never previously worked in property.

Zoopla's launch also came at a time when, Chesterman admits, 'the UK was not short of property portals'. Rightmove was already listing more than a million homes for sale or rent; Findaproperty and Primelocation had another 400,000 each. But Chesterman thought he could do better. 'The offerings were all very similar, and hadn't progressed much over the seven or eight years since they were first established during the early days of the internet.' It was when the entrepreneur started looking for a home to buy himself that he had the idea to start the site. 'I knew enormous amounts of property data had become publicly available as a result of the internet, but they were so hard to access.

'I was staying up half the night building spreadsheets of comparable properties and implied appreciation rates to figure out how much to offer on a house.' That was the catalyst for developing Zoopla. 'I saw an opportunity to combine property listings with sold price information, current value estimates and local market data, to build more than just a property search facility.'

Film star success

Chesterman knew the internet. He had previously co-founded film rental business ScreenSelect, which merged with Lovefilm to become Europe's largest DVD rental business, before being sold to Amazon for some £200 million. Both Lovefilm and Zoopla were, Chesterman says, 'founded with the basic objective of dramatically improving the consumer experience.' And, as with Zoopla, the entrepreneur hadn't known the film rental market before entering it. 'It can be an advantage to be an outsider – you see things with fresh eyes', he says. 'Not having worked within an industry previously should not be a constraint to developing and executing a good idea.'

According to Chesterman, that's even true when it comes to starting an online business with little techy know-how. Spreadsheets aside, he declares: 'I am not technically inclined at all.' So he sought out a co-founder. 'A partner should be someone that has different and complementary skills from your own', he says. 'Not your best friend or ex-work colleague who thinks the same, but someone who you can bounce ideas off, yet who still has the same work ethic, dedication and passion to pull off the vision for the business.' Chesterman approached Simon Kain, 'a technical wizard' who had worked as chief technology officer at Lovefilm.

Kain liked the idea behind Zoopla and agreed to become co-founder. 'Then the hard work began.' Listing and providing current, instant valuations for every home in the UK involved 'complex algorithms, data collection mechanisms and processing tools', Chesterman explains. When he wasn't up all hours number crunching, he was organising investment. 'The success of Lovefilm and being a "repeat" entrepreneur with a track record no doubt played a part in our ability to secure funding', he says. 'Investors often back the team as much as the idea.' More important than that, Chesterman believes, was the fact that his proposition was 'unique'. In a seed funding round, private equity group Atlas Ventures put in £1.5 million. Chesterman also put together an advisory board, with members coming from backgrounds including the Bank of England, British Property Federation, Lovefilm and Amazon.

All nighters

With cash in the bank and a team set up, work began on building Zoopla – so-named because 'we wanted something different, non-descriptive and non-limiting', he explains. 'The only times in my life I have ever pulled "all-nighters" were either cramming for school exams or working on a start-up', says Chesterman. 'And I've done more of those in the past ten years then I ever did at school. But if you love what you do and believe in what you are building then it is well worth the effort.' Days – and nights – were spent juggling site design, working on the maths at the backend, and speaking to estate agencies. Chesterman invited agents to list properties for free for a limited trial; later, they either had to pay fixed monthly subscriptions to advertise their listings, or pay per lead.

Zoopla launched in January 2008, with some paid advertising on Google, plus word-of-mouth referrals and PR. 'We tapped into a national obsession with property values and the nosey aspect of being able to see the values and sold prices paid for every home – yours or anyone else's', says Chesterman. Media interest was particularly strong around ideas like 'TemptMe!', where homeowners could list a price that would incite them to sell, and potential buyers could post a non-binding offer. Other talking points included Zoopla's 'property rich list', showing the priciest road in England (that's Kensington Palace Gardens, at an average of £28 million) and cheapest (Voelas Street, Liverpool: average price £30,500.) Users flocked, with over a million visitors per month before Zoopla was a toddler.

Then along came the recession – and the housing market crash. It was bad timing for Zoopla, which had been intending to raise more cash. 'Raising further funds in 2008, especially for a property-related business, was challenging', Chesterman admits. 'But since our product was innovative and had gained a lot of traction, we managed to buck the trends.' Zoopla managed to raise a total of nearly £9 million. 'We pushed forward, whilst others pulled back. Great businesses are often built during hard times', says Chesterman. 'Despite the property market down-turn, consumers still wanted more relevant information and transparency, and advertisers wanted to ensure real return on their marketing investment.'

Splurge

Zoopla's successful fundraising meant Chesterman could shop for some recession-era bargains. He spent 2009 buying two longer-established online property businesses, ThinkProperty.com from Guardian Media Group and PropertyFinder.co.uk from News International – 'businesses that had received over £40 million of investment from their former owners in the preceding three years', Chesterman points out proudly. 'Without the recession, it is unlikely that either of those businesses would have been available to acquire, and certainly not at a price we could afford.'

The team spent a summer absorbing their two purchases – which together had 3.2 monthly million visitors – into the site. Zoopla used cloud computing platforms to save money on servers and provide unlimited scalability. That became more important as Zoopla used its acquisitions to build a listings service. It quickly signed a deal with three property behemoths – Countrywide, LSL Property Services and Connells Group – who agreed to advertise their properties on Zoopla and provide marketing support in their 2000 high street branches. The website today lists over 550,000 properties from more than 8500 agent branches in the UK.

Zoopla's principle revenues now come from listing fees from agents and developers; extra earnings come from advertising and selling data to third parties. From its launch with a handful of employees in 2008 the business now has more than 90 staff. Zoopla receives over 10 million visitors and 80 million page views on its site per month.

Chesterman's ambition remains unharnessed. Zoopla has launched an iPhone and Android app and is working on an iPad version in its bid to become the top property website in the country. 'Online property continues to grow as a segment – over 90% of UK consumers now start their property search online, and property advertisers are shifting their spend from traditional print media to online as a result', says Chesterman, who is now 41. 'The appeal of an online business to me is the ability to start with a clean sheet of paper and build something entirely from scratch that is completely different – but still with the ability to tinker with and continuously improve it.'

Fact box: Zoopla

Launch: January 2008

Revenues: £8.1 million in 2010. Projected revenues for 2011: £14 million

Staff: 92

Top tip: 'If you have a good idea, go for it – never be afraid to try just because it hasn't been done before.'

Chapter 6

GOCOMPARE

For many, just the phrase 'go compare' is enough to lodge in one's head for a week the warblings of opera singer, Gio Compario, about the comparison site 'where the wise go to economise'. Indeed, Gio has directed huge traffic and brand success to the insurance and financial services aggregator that he's named after. But the mustachioed man is not the driving force behind the website that brought in a £30 million profit last year. That's Hayley Parsons, a Welsh entrepreneur who left school at 16 to work in the insurance industry, and found she quite liked it.

Parsons' dad advised her to start up a local hairdressing business when she quit school. But that wasn't her cup of tea. Instead, she secured a job making endless cups of the stuff as an office junior at a local insurance broker. A few promotions and job moves later, Parsons heard about a new insurance firm starting up nearby in Cardiff. That was Admiral Group, where she applied for a post, and ended up staying for 14 years.

There, Parsons was part of the team that launched Confused. com, the comparison site. Her story proves to web entrepreneurs that a business idea doesn't always have to be disruptive or new – it just has to do things differently. 'My role at Confused was to convince insurers that price comparison sites were the future – which was easier said than done at the time', Parsons recalls. 'I accumulated a great deal of knowledge, far more insight than any amount of desk research could have done.' But concerned with what she perceived as comparison sites' emphasis on 'pure price, rather than content', Parsons decided that she could do better. She wanted to create a site that focused on displaying the product features of an insurance policy, as well as prices. The result was Gocompare.com.

'You could say it was a light-bulb moment, but it was more about the realisation that I could go and start something myself, rather than staying and feeling frustrated with things', she explains. Parsons approached fellow Confused colleagues, Lee Griffin, Dan Cassell, Susie Bradshaw, Chris Davies and Dave Harvey, and in 2006 they all quit their jobs and converged around Parsons' kitchen table at her home in Newport to finesse the idea behind GoCompare. The latter four colleagues were 'the technical guys who wrote the code and got the website up and running', Parsons explains, whilst she and Griffin concentrated on wooing insurers.

GoCompare's initial funding came from a £1.5 million loan from Tom Duggan, an insurance industry veteran. 'It was surprisingly easy to get the funding', says Parsons. 'I've worked my entire adult life in insurance, and worked hard to establish valuable contacts. That matters a great deal when setting up a business.'

Parsons used that cash injection to build the site, pay early salaries and promote the brand amongst consumers. Its monetisation strategy was to make the website free to use by consumers, with the insurance companies and financial product providers listed on its site paying when a sale had been made. 'The early days were the most difficult', says Parsons. 'Building a highly-recognisable consumer brand from scratch was a daunting challenge.'

Grow or die

Heavy marketing costs meant GoCompare posted an £8.8 million loss in its first year in business, but that halved 12 months later to £4.1 million. Then Parsons heard that Tesco was planning to enter the price comparison market. 'That caused us some concern', she says. 'We thought "right, we can either carry on as we are and get muscled out, or try to raise more capital and really go for it."' GoCompare chose the latter, and Parsons secured a £30 million loan from Peter Wood, founder of insurer Esure, to finance a step-up in ambition. 'It paid off', says Parsons. 'We were able to build a brand that could compete with the previous market-leaders. We focused on how consumers could arm themselves with enough information to make an informed choice.' The GoCompare team had developed a quote engine that would display a range of additional information 'so that people knew what they were getting for their money – voluntary and compulsory excesses, courtesy cars, personal injury cover and more. We focused on that', says Parsons, 'and it took our competitors a long time to change their ways and catch up with us.' In the meantime, the GoCompare site roared ahead. By 2009, the business made a £12.1 million pre-tax profit, whilst a year later that had almost tripled to £30.1 million.

That man who sings opera . . .

The site's biggest cost has always been – and remains – advertising. 'We operate in a very competitive market place where brand awareness can make or break you, so we need to ensure that we are always top of people's minds when they're searching for insurance and other financial products online', says Parsons. 'Competition is a big challenge. The big four comparison sites

– GoCompare, Moneysupermarket, Compare The Market and Confused – all have to work hard to develop their brands and stand out from the crowd.'

That's where Gio Compario came in. The advertising campaign – which was the brainchild of Sian and Chris Wilkins, a husband and wife advertising team who also created the infamous Sheilas for Sheilas' Wheels – launched in August 2009. 'The challenge was to make sure that when people received their car insurance renewal letter, their first thought would be "GoCompare,"' says Parsons. 'I told Chris and Sian that I wanted a campaign that would stick in people's minds. I think it's safe to say that, with Gio, we got just that.'

Since introducing the opera singer's ads, GoCompare has seen a 60% increase in quote volumes, and a 450% uplift in brand awareness. It now provides over two million insurance quotes a month. 'We're all very pleased with how Gio has been received', says Parsons, unsurprisingly. 'Yes, some people find him annoying, but that's just because the campaign airs so often.' As well as TV and radio, GoCompare uses online advertising, including paid search, online banner ads, affiliate marketing and Twitter, Facebook and YouTube to build brand awareness and communicate with customers.

GoCompare paid back the £30 million loan to Esure in 2010; since then the business has been growing organically.

The people

'There's no way I could have achieved what I have without the support of the GoCompare team – in fact, the secret to my success is that I have surrounded myself with people that are much better than me', says Parsons on her recruitment policy.

'I'm very aware of my strengths and weaknesses. Having the right team lets me concentrate on growing the business, safe in the knowledge that, operationally, everything is being looked after.'

On hiring and firing, Parsons says she focused on picking the best talent, and worried about what to do with it later on. 'The people who work at Gocompare.com are crucial to the business', she says. 'In many cases we found the people we wanted, and created roles for them. As an entrepreneur, if you're working inhumane hours and never getting through your "to do" list, you've probably put off hiring people for a little too long.'

Parsons has built her own working day around her family and two sons. 'I arrive at the office before 9 a.m. after dropping my eldest son off at school, and start each day by looking at the numbers from the previous day before a catch-up with senior managers', she explains. 'I'm usually home before 7 p.m. each day. It's difficult to run a rapidly-growing company and a household without some help, and I've always been adamant that my sons should be picked up from school by one of their parents', she says. 'So we made the decision that Mark, my partner, would quit his job as the sales and marketing director of a busy printing firm and stay at home. It wasn't an easy decision to make but we're all glad we did.'

Looking to the future, GoCompare is now looking at diversifying into new product areas, as well as capitalising on the growth in smart phones. 'We're looking at enabling people to shop around on the hoof', says Parsons. Rumours are swirling of a potential acquisition, but the insurance entrepreneur says she 'loves working at GoCompare' and 'can't imagine not being here.'

Opportunity knocks

Still, Parsons believes the web still offers huge new business opportunities. 'Anyone setting up a business, regardless of what it is, should not underestimate the power of the internet', she says. 'I heard something recently that sums up how important it is to our daily lives now: "we used to be told to think before we speak, now we Google before we Tweet." Most people start looking for products and services using a search engine now, and if you can't be found online you could be missing a huge number of customers.

'I'd advise wannabe entrepreneurs to use the internet to try to identify a target market – who is being underserviced and just screaming out for something new or better than what is already on offer? Can you pull together a team to satisfy this demand? If you can, you're well on your way.

'I still can't believe that we've gone from a bunch of people sitting in my house to a company that employs over one hundred people in just four and a half years. The most important thing before taking the plunge and setting up your own business is to understand your worst-case scenario. If you're leaving a secure job to set up a business and it fails, the chances are you'll have a strong enough background and CV to get another job, so it's not too risky. Once you've made the decision to do it, go for it and don't look back.'

Fact box: GoCompare

Launch: November 2006

Revenues: Jumped 36% in 2010 to £101.5 million, from £74.9 m in 2009. Profit almost tripled from £12.1 million to £30.1 million.

Staff: 101

Top tip: 'Don't be afraid to make mistakes.'

CHAPTER 7

GROUPON / MYCITYDEAL

When Christopher Muhr, one of the founders of the international group discount buying site Groupon, heard about this book, he begged me to do one thing. 'Please', he said, 'you've got to highlight the entrepreneur's big problem in London: finding something to eat late at night.' It didn't sound like the world's most urgent issue, but Muhr was adamant. 'It's strange', he agreed. 'You're in this huge metropolis with millions of people, but, there's nowhere at all to eat after 10 p.m. I spent most of the many nights I worked on my site having to fight with the junkies around King's Cross station to get to Burger King before it closed. If you missed that, you were in trouble.'

London's dearth of late-night eateries made life, Muhr maintains, 'very difficult for a start-up.' But he laughs, because his success at helping to build deal website MyCityDeal into a business with revenues of over £100 million in little over a year shows a diet of burgers and Mars Bars hardly held him back.

Muhr, who is 30 and from Germany, started his career in investment banking. But he didn't last long. 'I was hopelessly unsuccessful, and ended up being fired at the end of my initial training programme', he explains. 'I wasn't very good at being managed.' From there, Muhr moved to Berlin, 'because it was such a start-up hub', and set up company eCareer – a subscription-

only online jobs board. It was backed by Germany's most pro-
lific start-up investors, the Samwer brothers, who have built up
a reputation creating clones of US online businesses. 'But again',
he says, 'It was very, very unsuccessful. Subscription models are
hard to scale in continental Europe.'

New direction

It was then that Muhr started noticing a great deal of noise
about a company called Groupon which was doing well in the
US. 'I read about it on [technology blog] TechCrunch, and
knew people in the US who were talking about it a lot', he says.
That was October 2009. The entrepreneur didn't think he could
create a particularly radical or improved version of the site, but
'just thought it was a pretty good business model, and that a
copycat site could work.' Muhr adds: 'I started to explore the
market, especially because I knew that Europe was very complex
for American companies to conquer. They didn't know how
Europe worked, and struggled with the red tape, and languages.
So I thought, what about building this idea in the European
market, and seeing how far we can go?'

Anyone looking to replicate a site that already exists needs, says
Muhr, to have a good eye for what works. 'You need to be able
to spot a well-functioning business model from a long way off',
he explains. 'If I see an interesting idea, I explain the business
model to my mum. And if she understands it in two minutes,
I consider it a good one. Groupon was one of those.'

The other crucial requirement on Muhr's list of how to create
a copycat site is speediness. 'If you single out a model you want
to go after, you can't allow anything to get in your way', he says.
'You don't have the time advantage that an innovator might
have – you need to be twice as aggressive in operations and

execution, work harder than anyone else, and put in more hours than anyone else.' Hence the reason why Muhr could be found prowling London's streets looking for food in the middle of what the rest of the city believed to be the night.

But first, he had to mine his contacts. Muhr had decided to start the site in London – 'the UK is one of the biggest markets in Europe, people like a good deal and London is a great pool for talent', he explains – so he began furious networking, before securing €4 million from three VCs – eVenture Capital Partners, Holtzbrinck Ventures and Rocket Internet, which belonged to the Samwer brothers. 'Since I'd worked with the same investors previously, they were willing to back me again', he says.

Muhr signed up his girlfriend and hordes of friends in Berlin to trawl the British online directory Yelp in order to start typing up lists of merchants who might offer him deals to sell. 'We put them into a huge Excel spreadsheet, then flew over to the UK around Christmas', he remembers. 'Then, we started cold calling retailers, restaurants, gyms – everyone possible. Initially it was crazy – there was a lot of overlap: because we had no list of who we'd already called, people were contacting the same people two or three times. It was completely chaotic.'

The team didn't find it easy to encourage businesses to agree to give away their goods at significant discount – potentially damaging their brand cache – to a site which didn't exist and had no members. 'It involved a lot of enthusiasm', says Muhr. 'If you're a start-up you're always going to need to get some business on board first, and that's the toughest part. You need to come across as someone who's very confident in your own ability, and you need to know where you want to be in some years to come. We had to act like we were there already, and tell people our vision – so we were saying, "we're going to be this big, we're investing this many millions of euros in marketing" – you have to act as if you're already there.'

Sprint finish

The first two people in MyCityDeal's dingy office in Gray's Inn Road in Kings Cross were Muhr and one of his former colleagues from Berlin, Benedikt Franke, who worked on operations. 'We hired 10 people within two weeks, the growth was extremely rapid', says Muhr. 'We went for young guys with no experience, who were on pretty basic salaries. Their job was to convince people that there was a bigger plan in the pipeline.'

Looking back, Muhr admits: 'It was scary. There were 12 people crammed into a tiny office, and a team in Berlin from eCareer who built a very basic website. It had a counter, for when we would upload a deal, and then the simplest possible transactional site behind it.

'It was a piece of shit, but it worked. As a copycat, you don't have the time to build the most sophisticated idea around. You just need something that can do what it needs to do. And ours did.'

The first company to sign up with a deal was a French restaurant. 'It was an OK deal, not great', Muhr explains. 'Our margin was rubbish, and I think we sold 20 vouchers. It was pretty disappointing, but at least it showed the idea worked, and people were interested.'

For the first six months of MyCityDeal's development, Muhr says he 'lived in the office.' His working day began at 7 a.m., and ran until 2 or 3 a.m. the following day. 'I had a drawer with all my belongings, and only left the office to sleep and shower once in a while, before quickly returning. There was no such thing as a weekend, and I didn't take a holiday for almost 16 months. It was a very intense time.

'As the founder of a start-up, especially when you replicate an existing business model and so need to stay on your toes all the time, that company becomes your whole world. It's your family, and the people working there become your only social interaction', says Muhr. 'Socially I lost out massively, I didn't have the time to talk to friends.'

But if Muhr's social networking wasn't going well, his business networking was. Every new daily deal the team secured and sold made it easier to do the same – and more successfully – the following day. Marketing was carried out through a mixture of 'crazily subsidised deals, and Facebook, Twitter, plus Google pay-per-click and ads in local newspapers.' But most of the money went on online promotion – 'as a web company I think that's where you have to look for most of your users', says Muhr. By April 2010, MyCityDeal was selling a few hundred units of offers each day. 'Then the key challenge became keeping everyone focused. With a lot of people under management you need really good management skills to keep the whole operation focused for a long time – and you need to do it in a way that staff don't feel over-managed.' Muhr's team had strong camaraderie. 'We developed these rituals, like we'd all "high five" everyone in the office when we hit certain targets, and make bets about how many of a particular deal we'd sell', says Muhr. 'Mostly, though, everyone was excited to be working there.'

Fish shortages

Growth accelerated astonishingly fast over the first year. A medieval banquet deal sold 1000, 'then suddenly we were selling

4000, then 10,000 offers per day', says Muhr. The site negoti-
ated a deal with cinema chain Cineworld to offer tickets to a
film for £1, and sold 50,000 in less than 24 hours. 'It showed
how much power there was in the model', Muhr believes. 'We
had subsidised the cost of the film tickets, but it really did show
how many people were excited about a good deal. We learnt
very quickly about how to structure offers, which worked best
for merchants, and which appealed most to consumers. At one
point, fish pedicures were so popular amongst our users that
the salons used up all the fish in the UK, and had to import
more from Scandinavia.'

At the start, Muhr admits he was 'super paranoid' about competition. 'Every day I looked at rival sites to see what they were
doing', he says. 'Initially I was convinced they were going to
outsmart us, but gradually I relaxed.' Then, by the middle of
2010, the predator became the prey. Muhr was contacted by
Andrew Mason, founder of Groupon, about meeting him for
talks. 'I had to rent out a conference room, because we didn't
have a single room that was suitable for a meeting like that,
and he flew over to London', the entrepreneur explains. 'When
Andrew turned up, he was pretty jetlagged and not really up
for conversation. But we sat in the small room and went through
the business, how we executed it, and the differences between
us and Groupon. I think we both realised very quickly that we
would gain from merging.'

A sale had always been on the cards, Muhr explains. 'I think
all entrepreneurs plan with the idea of an exit – you don't build
a business because it's something you want to do for the rest
of your life. Over time I started thinking about values, our
revenues and what they could grow to.' But the entrepreneur
now wishes he'd had 'a bit more faith in the business. We could
have built it to a different size, and not had to sell to anyone.
I didn't quite realise how powerful the site had become.'

At the time, however, Muhr was still worried about competition and how he would build the scale to expand. He believed a tie-up with Groupon was 'a perfect fit', and so did Mason. The American and his Groupon board spent what is reported to be around $100 million snapping up MyCityDeal in the UK, as well as its equivalent sites in other European countries, which had also been funded by the Samwer's incubator fund Rocket Internet. Today, Muhr is a senior vice president of sales at Groupon, living in Chicago, and a shareholder in the merged entity. 'I wouldn't have left even if they'd have tried to get rid of me', he says. 'I'm still having too much fun.'

Fact box: Groupon

Launch: February 2010

Revenues: Circa £100 million for the year before sale

Staff: 150 at point of sale

Top tip: 'Focus on what matters – the essential things that make your business survive – for Groupon, it's deals and customers. Ignore everything else.'

CHAPTER 8

SPAREROOM

Rupert Hunt moved to London to become a rock star. It was 1997, he was in a band called Leonard – 'it was indie, alt rock type stuff, with influences such as Pavement and R.E.M' – and he was living in 'a crummy flat above a van hire shop on the noisy approach to the Blackwall tunnel. But I loved it.' Yet despite radio play by both the late DJ John Peel and Bob Geldof, Hunt's dreamed-of record deal never arrived. Luckily for him, inspiration of another sort did.

When he moved down from his family's home on a farm in Cheshire to London, Hunt had struggled to find somewhere to live. 'I was', he says, 'amazed at how difficult it was to find rooms in shared houses in London. The information available ranged from sketchy to non-existent – and I thought, surely the web could do this better.'

It could: 14 years on, over 2.3 million registered users have visited his flatshare website SpareRoom, and revenues this year are set to approach £2 million. Yet Hunt was no tech guru. He had dabbled in web design whilst at university, studying for a degree in pop music at Leeds University. There, he had opted to take a module in the new field of web design 'because I was curious', he says.

After graduating, Hunt struggled to find work and signed on to the dole, then worked in Tesco as he waited for his big break in music. To earn more money, he answered an ad in listings paper *Loot*, from someone seeking help in maintaining a website. That eventually led to Hunt landing a full-time web development job, working on sites for musical instrument shops and a sportswear group. But, during the daily grind, Hunt's problems finding a flatshare kept spinning around his brain, and then sparked up an idea. 'I decided to set up a basic, online noticeboard for flatshares, and called it intoLondon.com.'

To his surprise, Hunt's spare-time project 'started to get pretty popular.' So he thought he'd see if users would pay for it. 'I decided to try charging people to use it – almost as an experiment', he says. 'But I also wanted to see whether I could generate some income and fund a bit more time to spend developing the idea – and my music.'

The sound of success

He quickly discovered Londoners were indeed happy to pay to access Hunt's hundreds of flatshare ads. Revenues slowly started to trickle in, and when they got up to £500 a month, Hunt decided to leave behind the London flat he'd found through his site, as well as his job and long-term girlfriend, and move back to his parents in Cheshire – 'thanks to my parents putting me up and feeding me', he chirps – to turn intoLondon.com into a commercial venture.

The venture was a one-man band run from a tiny shed on Hunt's dad's farm. The first colleagues were 'about 1000 spiders.' Hunt was terrified of spiders – so the working day was frequently interrupted by him running out of the shed door, 'flapping my arms around'. When the arachnids stayed away, it was fingers to the grindstone. 'I did everything to start with, the entire site was written by me – large portions of it are still my code', says Hunt. That meant there was no need for funding, although the entrepreneur used a credit card to pay for living costs.

IntoLondon's existing success negated the need for market research. 'I knew the market was there and that nobody was really addressing its needs', says Hunt. 'It made more sense for me to learn by simply getting into it – testing the market is far more useful than any list of stats.' First up was a name change to make his website nationally scaleable. SpareRoom sprung to mind. 'It says what it does in pretty simple terms – I'm not a fan of abstract company names, especially online', says Hunt, who is 36. 'If your users can tell what the site does simply from the name then you've already got over the first hurdle to getting them onboard.'

He designed the site himself, 'mostly from instinct'. Hunt poetically explains: 'A website is like a novel – you start with a first draft, then keep on rewriting the bits that don't work.' The only difference, he concedes, 'is that a website's audience keeps changing so you never finish rewriting.' SpareRoom's monetization plan was inspired by the early social networking site Friends Reunited. 'It was charging £5 for a lifetime membership, enabling their users to make contact with each other. So the first product on my site was "lifetime full membership" for £5, which allowed users to contact the latest ads seven days before everyone else', says Hunt. 'After a month or two, an old friend of my father's was visiting the farm and I told him how surprised I'd been at the level of sales. He asked, 'why don't you change it to a limited time period so you can get renewals too?'. That was a pivotal moment. It seems obvious now, but back then, very few sites were charging for online content, so the idea seemed audacious.'

Hunt developed a routine of settling into his work shed at 7 a.m. and working till 9 p.m., seven days a week. He still does. 'Running a business as busy as SpareRoom takes over your life, but I've never had a problem motivating myself. I think if you're not living to work as well as working to live, you're probably in the wrong line of work.'

Growth

Initially it was just Hunt in what he calls the 'spider shed' but, in 2003, he bumped into an old childhood friend, and met his girlfriend Gemma Craft. 'I mentioned what I was doing with the site, and she said she worked for a lettings agent in Manchester. At the time, I was getting a bit bogged down with answering user emails and calls, which was taking me away from the important development work on the site, so I asked her to come and work for me.' Craft started off working one evening per week plus Saturdays, but Hunt soon decided to take the plunge and offer her a job. 'The thought of offering a full-time, salaried job seemed pretty scary, but was definitely one of the best decisions I ever made', he says.

Hunt later recruited a part-time customer service assistant, but he avoided hiring anyone to help with development until 2008, nearly five years after launch. He now believes he waited too long to recruit staff to SpareRoom – 'almost getting to the point where we couldn't physically cope without more people' and adds: 'knowing when to recruit is one of the hardest things of all – especially when you've been the entire team yourself for a while.

'If you take someone on with specialist skills too early you risk not having enough for them to do. But too late and you find yourself struggling to keep up with the competition – and your own workload.' The entrepreneur believes it's crucial to avoid being so under-manned that customer service levels fall. 'When you get that right, it fuels great word-of-mouth marketing – probably our most useful tool these days. It's probably a bit over the top to say customer service is the new marketing, but if you keep that in mind it'll help.'

Shoestring budget

Since starting up SpareRoom, Hunt's only external funding has been a £20,000 loan to buy out a competitor, flatshare.com, in 2004. 'Looking back it probably wasn't as necessary to do that as I thought at the time, but I was far more concerned about competition back then than I am now. Buying flatshare.com has paid for itself many times over now though, and the loan was paid back pretty quickly as we started making a bigger profit', he adds.

'People presume you need loads of capital to start up a business but that's simply not true – especially online where costs like manufacturing, premises and stock holding can be avoided. Not taking on someone else's money forces you to be more creative and, at the same time, more cautious in how you spend. Funding doesn't guarantee success and you learn the important lessons more quickly if it's your own money.'

SpareRoom began funding itself in the second half of 2004. Turnover for the year to July 2005 was just over £100,000 with profits of £30,000. Although the site is free to use, around a fifth of SpareRoom's users opt to pay £9 a week for an upgraded ad, with prices falling proportionately for more weeks up to £69 for a year. The site doesn't have banner advertising 'if people are paying to use our service why should they be bombarded with other people's services while they do?', asks Hunt.

Nowadays the site's biggest costs are paying for Google Adwords – they totted up to a bill of around £210,000 last year – and salaries for 26 employees. 'Our aim is to provide the same level of service and safety using SpareRoom as you'd get from a good retail outlet, so we have staff in the office seven days-a-week, answering phone calls and emails and moderating listings by hand to keep scams off the site', says Hunt. 'Just because websites don't come into contact with their customers in the way that shops do, that's no excuse to skimp on customer care.'

The entrepreneur began withdrawing a salary for himself a year after setting up the site, paying himself around £40,000, 'but I have recently given myself a small rise!', he adds. 'Still, I'm not sure if it's market rate – I suspect if I went out to recruit an MD to take over from me it might cost me a fair bit more.'

Making some noise (quietly)

Whilst SpareRoom's name was passed between flat-seekers' and the site's numbers slowly increased, Hunt thought about ways to spread its name. 'If you create the best possible product or service you can, word of mouth will do more for you than endless advertising, but they do need to find out about you in the first place', he says. Search engine optimisation was his first strategy. 'To begin with, I was really successful with it, but it's changed such a lot over the years and is now extremely difficult – it can take six months to a year to appear anywhere on the listings, never mind in the top results. That said, SEO is still the most important and affordable kind of marketing for most online businesses, and pay-per-click is fast and powerful. You can spend as much or as little as you like, have complete control over where you send visitors and, most importantly, you can track what works, so by using trial and error and measuring results you can hone your marketing in a relatively inexpensive way.'

Despite the noise about social networking, Hunt hasn't found it to be the most effective form of marketing for his business. 'Twitter has helped us with monitoring what people say about SpareRoom as well as with networking with other businesses, but I think it's marginal in terms of driving traffic', he says. Hunt believes SpareRoom's best marketing campaign has been its Speed Flatmating idea – speed dating for flatmates ('meet loads of potential new flatmates in the time it would take you to travel to and look round a single flat and discover you wouldn't want to share with the people there anyway') and there are now 15 a month in London. As well as a marketing method, the meet-ups have also become a crucial route for Hunt and his team to receive feedback about SpareRoom's functionality. 'As a website, you may have hundreds of thousands of people passing through your doors every month but, unlike running a shop, you never see them. Talking to people at our Speed Flatmating events means we get insights we'd never get in a million years otherwise', says Hunt.

But publicity wasn't always easy to deal with for Hunt and his early founding team. 'Back in 2007, we'd decided to push our PR activities a bit harder and, out of the blue, got a call from a producer on the BBC Radio 2 Chris Evans show. One of our competitors had put out a press release on people taking in lodgers, but weren't answering their phone so they asked us to do a live interview on the show.' Hunt and his team had 'a long, terrified conversation about which of us was going to do the interview.' In the end they settled on 'the least petrified one of us', one of the site's directors, Matt Hutchinson. 'Thankfully it went OK and Matt has continued to be the spokesperson for the company. You do need someone in-house who is confident and comfortable presenting your message to the media. Even if you hire a PR agency, they won't know your business as well as you do.'

Code red

In a bid to cut costs – and save his own time – Hunt began outsourcing some of his site's coding to a developer but, he says, 'doing so was a mistake. After several months of coding, the guy said he wanted to get a regular job and give up on the project. I had the choice of finding another coder to take it over, or offering him a job. Stupidly I did the latter. Because he wasn't local, he worked from home and the situation got worse and worse. The project barely saw the light of day, and I was close to £100,000 worse off by the time he left.

'My basic rule of thumb now is to avoid outsourcing in almost all situations. If you can, instead of outsourcing, learn to do it yourself. It deepens your understanding of what's going on in the business and means the knowledge is kept in-house.' Hunt flags up the example of SpareRoom's recent iPhone app. 'We were considering outsourcing that but one of our developers knew enough to get started with it and he learned as he went along. We now have a fantastic app, designed and built by people who know our business and the needs of our users. And we have the skills within the company to build further apps.'

The future – and beyond

Hunt has just launched SpareRoom in New York from his base in the UK. 'A freelancer there is helping with marketing, but we're doing everything else from over here', he says. 'The similarities between New York and London in terms of people needing accommodation are pretty obvious so it seemed the ideal opportunity to try another market. Beyond that, there are obvious next moves in the US as well as Australia. We're also keen to look at Europe soon.'

But Hunt has no plans to sell up or quit, despite having being made a multimillion-pound offer for 49% of the site last year. 'I think it's a shame that everyone seems to have an exit strategy from day one these days', he says. 'Some people's idea of business is to create something and sell it for as much as possible, as soon as possible. One of the reasons I love SpareRoom is that it's my company – I enjoy seeing it grow and being hands-on on a daily basis. One thing that got me hooked on the internet as a means of doing things was the idea that anything was possible.'

Indeed Hunt's site is growing fast. SpareRoom is now the eighth busiest property website in the UK, and is in the top 0.05% most-visited sites in the UK. 'This', Hunt admits, 'still astounds me on a daily basis. It doesn't seem all that long ago I was stacking shelves in Tesco and coding in my spare time.'

Fact box: SpareRoom

Launch: intoLondon,1999; SpareRoom, 2004; Spare-Room New York, 2011.

Revenues: £1.5 million for the year to August 2010

Staff: 26

Top tip: 'Ideas are important but ten a penny – execution is what will make you successful or not. Work hard and be nice to people. Roll your sleeves up, take a deep breath and get on with it. Good luck.'

CHAPTER 9

MADE.COM

It's the classic example of a business born out of frustration. Ning Li wanted a new sofa. He was 28, working as a banker, and wanted to splash some cash on a piece of designer leather furniture. He shopped the home furnishing stores, eventually found a sofa of choice, and just was about to stick the £3000 bill on his credit card when he happened to talk to an old school friend from China, the country he grew up in.

'I just mentioned to my friend, who I'd sat next to every day at primary school, that I was about to buy this sofa', says Li. 'And he told me that he had just taken over his parents' furniture-making factory – and that they had won the contract to make the exact sofa I was about to buy.'

Li's friend informed him that his Chinese factory was paid £250 for his £3000 sofa. So, once Li had bought his furniture direct from his contact in China (for less than 10% of the retail price), he started looking into furniture pricing and its journey from drawing board to living room. That's when he discovered that big-ticket furniture passed through up to ten different agents on its journey from factory in China to showroom in western Europe, each adding a mark-up. 'Then I realised that the internet – which had disrupted so many big industries – hadn't touched the furniture business', says Li. 'It hadn't really changed much since Ikea tackled pricing, and that was more than 50 years ago.'

Sofa so good . . .

So Li decided to quit his job as a banker, and gave himself a frantic three-week deadline to organise a founding team for his start-up. He wanted to have developers and funding both in place to launch Made.com, a website cutting out the high-street middleman to sell furniture made all over the world direct to the public, in weeks – because he believed speed was crucial.

'I'm not techy at all, sadly', he says, 'and I knew we'd have technological problems launching the site, but I was sure that for web businesses you would need to be fast. Sometimes speed is more important than finding flawless code. It's better to make a site, test, fail, and test again, but do so very quickly, because it's so easy for people to copy an idea online. It's often only if you get in there first and build a brand that you've got a chance of success.'

Li began frantically networking to build a team. 'I was the idea man, but I signed up two co-founders, Julien Callede, chief operating officer who was to manage the supply chain, and Chloe MacIntosh, the creative hand', he explains. The trio quickly realised they were missing one thing: 'none of us', Li sheepishly admits, 'knew much about furniture.' Designers were beginning to send through ideas, but the founding team had no idea what would sell. Their solution to the problem was crowdsourcing – inviting consumers to decide what the Made.com website would offer for sale.

'We couldn't afford to have a buyer travelling the world's design fairs but, since we needed to know what customers wanted, we decided to put up a voting page on the website, asking which items of furniture they wanted to buy', says Li. Registered users would tick 'love' or 'loathe' next to products like the Stroller desk (£299), Piggy Bag bean bag (£59) or Jazz Club leather chair (£199), and only the most popular options would go on sale, with a 10-day window for orders. Customers would pay upfront, and Made.com would then place an exact order from the manufacturer, cutting out the need for a warehouse. 'Which meant', says Li, 'we could offer lower prices.'

Networking essentials

The entrepreneur did some number crunching and found he could promise discounts of between 50% and 80% on furniture from cupboards and sideboards to sofas and even retro-style bikes. He believed the quality would be akin to the likes of the Conran Store and Roche Bobois, since he was using the same suppliers, and focused on that high-end concept in marketing plans.

Idea fleshed out and ready to run, Li still needed cash to pay for salaries and promotional activity. The final piece in his start-up puzzle fell into place when he met Brent Hoberman, founder of lastminute.com, through a friend. Hoberman knew the furniture industry through his own home design site mydeco.com, and put Made.com's business plan to fellow members of his investment fund PROfounders Capital, who include Bebo founder Michael Birch, and Marc Simoncini, who owns Match.com's European operations.

The PROfounders' backers liked Li's idea and put up £2.5 million for a minority stake in the business. 'The fact that this team – all mostly entrepreneurs in a previous life – backed

Made helped a lot', says Li. 'They brought not only money but also expertise.'

Hoberman's MyDeco site had a spare room in its Notting Hill headquarters. 'So we moved in', says Li. 'It was small, with room for only three desks. It was very intense.' When I first visited Made.com's office, a year after launch, Li had a lair of rooms, all sprinkled with sleek tables, chairs and bean bags from the Made.com site, and employees rushing around everywhere. But at launch Made.com had just five staff: the founding three plus Andy Skipper, a chief technology officer ('a techy who can also talk business – a rare beast!', says Li) plus Win Kwok, art director. 'We worked days and nights, and weekends of course, to launch the site', says Li. The brief he gave Skipper was 'make me a website so simple that my mum understands how to use it' – Li wanted it to be very simple and functional, 'yet elegant'. All of the development took place in-house.

The entrepreneur found hiring his first staff difficult. 'In the beginning, as an unknown start-up, you can't pay big fat salaries, so you have to accept giving away some equity and paying partly in shares or stock options', he says. 'No entrepreneur likes to be diluted – but sometimes it's better to have a lesser stake of a bigger cake.' Recruiting staff is, Li concedes, a 'bit of a chicken and egg problem – when the company is on track and making some noises in the industry, it's easier to hire, but you need the right people to get you to that stage. It's definitely better to spend time and money on hiring the right person – otherwise you'll just have to spend more later.'

Take off

Made.com's launch was tentative. 'We advertised with Google Adwords and promoted the site on Facebook and Twitter, but didn't make a major splash and, during the first two weeks, we were only getting one or two orders a day', he explains. Li needed to sell close to 80 sofas to fill one container for shipping – and he'd told customers to expect their goods within 8–12 weeks, but momentum was slow.

Suddenly, however, 'there was a tipping point', says Li. 'People started talking about us – in the media, on social networks, in the real world – and the orders rushed in.' Six months after start-up, Li starting paying himself a salary. Another six months down the line, Made.com was receiving 500,000 visits a month, and selling one shipping container – full of furniture worth £25,000 – every day.

The site jumped on the slogan 'prices stripped bare' and frequently photographed artfully-naked torsos draped around its tables and chairs for the website. Its main marketing was, however, word-of-mouth. 'As a start-up, you need to use happy customers to spread the word', says Li. 'You can't afford to go after big guys like John Lewis or Ikea in marketing or advertising budget. You just can't beat them there. You can, however, compete with them and beat them by offering a better product or service – which requires more creativity and dedica-tion.' A referral programme means Made.com surfers who publish the fact that they 'like' one of its products on Facebook receive a £20 credit for every purchase made by a friend as a result.

Nowadays, Made.com is shipping £50,000-worth of furniture every day, with designers from Italy to India pitching ideas to get on the site. Li and his team receive up to 100 furniture designs every month; around 10 of those are put up for a public vote, and the two or three most popular then go on sale. Designers earn nothing upfront, but receive a 5% royalty on sales.

'It's only recently that I've managed to get some rhythm into my working day – and I just took my first holiday from work in two years', says Li. 'At the start, work was literally 24 hours per day. When I wasn't in the office – usually from 10 a.m. till the early hours of the morning – I was on my phone, or building my network or handling manufacturers.' Li now visits China at least once a month: he has set up one office and factory in Shanghai, and another in Guangzhou, a short flight away, which together employ 20 people in manufacturing, sourcing, quality control and management. 'Doing business in China requires a lot of patience', says Li. 'The Chinese love to work with long-term partners. It's crucial to focus on building up relationships first, then business comes after. That's the rule.'

Expansion

With revenues going above £2 million in just Made.com's second year of business, it's little surprise that Li and his team have already worked out plans to scale up the site. They're thinking internationally – with a launch in the US expected soon, after a second round of fundraising – and are currently working on Made.biz, a site for business owners and office supply managers to buy office furniture at wholesale prices. In January 2012, Made raised another £6 million in a second round of funding.

It is, Li says, 'too early' to think about an exit. 'But I know that I need to feel passionate and creative enough about the site to get up in the morning', he adds. 'For the moment I am. Maybe some day, when we become a multi-national, and I don't feel like I'm the right person to manage the business anymore, I'll think of exit. But until then, I'll stay right here.'

Fact box: Made.com

Launch: April 2010

Staff: 40

Revenues: £5 million+ for 2010

Top tip: 'Ask your friends and family for their opinions of your business idea, and do market studies – but the most important thing to trust is your instinct.'

Chapter 10

MOO.COM

The idea behind Moo – a business card website that now has hundreds of thousands of customers in 180 countries, came to founder Richard Moross when he was working at a design agency. He told his then-boss about the idea, offering to fund it himself and give the advertising maestro equity in the business, in exchange for a free desk to work from. His boss said no. 'Facepalm', as Moross, who decided to quit his day job and give entrepreneurship a try anyway puts it, 'I'm pretty sure he regrets that now.'

Moross was 25 when he first started creating a website, in 2004. He'd never had ambitions to start a business but, after leaving university and spending six months working in finance at the BBC, his best friend's brother asked him to get involved with his new dotcom. The site was called sorted.com, aimed at discovering secret places in your neighbourhood. Moross was hired alongside 20 other young graduates. 'I learnt sales, coding and marketing', he says. 'I wasn't very good at anything but got a sense of the skills involved in making a website.'

He stayed for 18 months, before it became clear Sorted.com wasn't quite sorted itself. 'The model couldn't survive: there were 19 people doing content and one doing sales – it should have been the other way round. It didn't make any money. But I was one of the first people through the door, and one of the last people to lock up. I learnt what failure feels like – and that, no matter how smart or nice you are or how good your idea is, if the market sticks two fingers up at you, you're either doomed – or you have to find some energy to turn it into something else.'

'Pleasure cards'

His next job was at the design company. 'My two years there, learning about strategy and branding, were a helpful contrast to the scrappy, everyone-does-everything environment of Sorted.com', says Moross. Then he had his big idea: shaking up the business card market, selling customers mini cards which would feature the web address of a microsite within his own site, where they could portray themselves or their business. 'A kind of early social networking', says Moross, who decided to name the site 'Pleasurecards.com'. It was supposed to sound like the opposite of business cards. 'It wasn't till much later that I realised just how awful the name was. I thought was being edgy . . .', Moross admits.

The entrepreneur had just taken on a mortgage and had very little savings, but nonetheless decided to quit the rat race and devote three months to working on his web idea. 'I didn't know anyone in the investment world, but started asking everyone I knew if they did', says Moross. 'Eventually my dad's business partner's neighbour's friend – it really was that convoluted – stepped forward.' He was Robin Klein, of angel investment firm the Accelerator Group, which had invested in 60 early stage companies, including lastminute.com, LastFM and Tweetdeck. After emails pinged back and forth, Klein invited Moross to a meeting at 7.30. Moross put him through a long presentation with a whopping 200 slides ('I later found out five would have done). But Klein was hooked, agreeing to put £150,000 into the business in return for what Moross describes as a 'meaningful' stake.

With the cash in the bank, he immediately swung into action, hiring an agency who he paid a flat fee to create a website, and agreeing terms with a London printer to create the cards. He then began to carry out his launch strategy: sending personalised sample cards to high-profile people who he regarded as 'influencers', telling them that the cards and their microsites were going to be the next big thing. 'That was a big mistake', says Moross. 'Never tell people things are cool – let them work that out.' But he had an even bigger problem: 'everyone hated Pleasure Cards. The feedback was awful. They didn't like the fact that the card was first about my website, and only second about them. I received streams of emails asking, "Can I personalise the cards with pictures and designs?" But I had to say no, as I didn't have the technological know-how or any money left to work it out.'

New start

Moross's business idea was drowning, but the Kleins threw him a rubber ring. They brought in VC Index Ventures and, together, they looked at how the business could change. 'You've got to have good advisors', Moross says today. 'It's so worth giving up a meaningful percentage of your business to investors just to have that experience around you. They will help you get the timing right about decisions like when to launch, and when to grow. They've been there, done that.'

Moross and his team came to the decision that Moo's physical 'minicards' were distinctive and popular and, instead of building their own social software, they should partner with other platforms where people already had blogs, online photos and avatars. The first link-up was with Wee World, a Scottish company which designed 'WeeMee' avatars. It paid Moross – who had by now renamed the company Moo ('it was short, funny, and memorable, and the domain name wasn't owned by a corporate so it was possible to buy') – to integrate its software into Moo's code. Moross beefed up his team, including an in-house developer, who accepted a half salary with the rest in equity: the total budget for all legal, development and staff costs at start-up was around £300,000. He signed up Stefan Magdalinski – founder of neighbourhood site Upmystreet.com – as chief technology officer and brought in a team of designers and technologists.

All that work meant that Moo customers would be able to personalise their cards, which were designed as half the size of normal business cards. As well as Wee World, Moross went on to develop lucrative partnerships with photo sites including Flickr, blogging giant LiveJournal, virtual world Second Life and social-networking site Bebo. Customers were given the opportunity to use up to 100 different photos and designs in each pack, with a different image on each card.

Spreading the word

The idea was gaining momentum. Moross talked to five of the fastest-growing social networking blogs at the time. 'They went crazy for the site, and that generated enough interest for a much higher investor commitment. In April 2006, VCs Atlas and Index together put in £3 million. Moross started paying himself a salary, and five months later, Moo was ready to be turned on. Magdalinski, deeply involved in the tech world, told 100 developer friends, including bloggers and other early-adopters, about the site. On launch day, the team nervously waited in Moo's first office, a 100 sq metre warehouse in Clerkenwell, north London. 'We were incredibly scared that no one would buy anything', says Moross. 'As it turned out, all the early adopters were in there, [influential blog] Boing Boing wrote a piece about us and, when we turned the site on at lunch time, it very quickly went down.' Since Moo's servers were 'pretty much in someone's front room', they couldn't cope with the demand.

But the techies resuscitated the servers, and Moross and his team stayed up for the whole launch night, with every card order projected onto a big board showing the designs, pictures and bios customers were ordering – all over the world. In the first week, card orders came in from more than 100 countries. Marketing was imaginative – like The Business Card Project, where small businesses were invited to send in pictures of their old business cards, and Moo picked the 'worst' 500 for a makeover – and growth was rapid. Revenues have, on average, doubled every year, although Moross refuses to specify exact earnings. New products launched, including greeting cards, sticker books, card holders, and postcards; when I met Moross in Moo's huge new Old Street office, there were 50 staff, and a manufacturing floor where all the printing now takes place in-house.

By 2009, Moross officially took his business to the US. North America had already grown to make up 45% of Moo's revenues when the site was based in London. 'But it wasn't environmentally friendly, quick or cheap', says Moross. So Moo opened in Rhode Island, and Moross promoted his VP of operations in London to open Moo Inc in the US. Today he speaks to him daily, as well as flying over the pond about ten times a year.

'People', says Moross when I ask for his key advice for wannabe entrepreneurs, 'get bogged down into thinking about the internet with a level of abstraction. Imagine your website as a bar. It will need a good design, and you'll need to make sure the first people through the door are cool, so that less cool people are then drawn in. You don't have to be cool yourself to make something cool, but you do need to know people who can tap into that cool world. So, for internet businesses, you don't need to be techy, or even to know the 10 top techy people, but you do need to know someone who does. With that and a good idea, you're on your way to success.'

Fact box: Moo

Launched: 2004

Revenues last year: '£10s of millions'

Staff: 80 in the US and UK

Top tip: 'Work hard. If you really, really, really work hard, you'll get somewhere. Without graft, you'll never get a web business off the ground.'

CHAPTER 11

ENTERNSHIPS

Oxford University was hosting one of its regular career fairs. Students were mingling with Magic Circle law firms, accountancy giants, banks, management consultancies and headhunters; many were stocking up on free pens, all were window shopping for a career. But second-year student Rajeeb Dey wasn't impressed. 'I looked at all work and internship opportunities, and thought: where do prospective entrepreneurs go?'

As president of the university's Entrepreneurship Society, Dey had learnt that the best way to learn about how to create a business – apart from doing so – was to work in a start-up. 'But the only roles we were exposed to on campus were those of blue chip corporations who were doing the graduate milk round', he says. 'The careers service didn't seem well-equipped to deal with start-ups or small businesses.'

Dey knew the opportunities were out there. He had become Oxford's go-to man on enterprise opportunities, with founders of start-ups getting in touch with him to ask if he knew a clever student who was techy, good at maths or an excellent writer to work as an intern. 'They lacked the brand awareness of someone like Goldman Sachs or PriceWaterhouseCoopers, so they weren't in a position to look directly', Dey explains.

He decided to start advertising the opportunities in the Entrepreneurship Society's weekly newsletter; after a while, he thought a website would offer an easily updateable match-making service.

So Dey convinced two student friends to design and create a basic website. He called it Enternships – 'people may initially think it's a typo', he explains, 'but that can be the start of a conversation around how an enternship is an entrepreneurial internship.' Dey started to list the placements and the site ticked along quietly but successfully as Dey concentrated on studying for his degree.

And then the economy imploded

Then came graduation day. It was 2008 when Dey tossed his mortarboard up in the air: Lehman Brothers, the investment bank, collapsed, global recession began to kick in – and the graduate unemployment market started to shrivel up. University leavers became more desperate for work, and small businesses were looking for ways to cut costs – but they still needed bright workers. Dey realised that his site might tap into a crucial need. 'A few hundred firms had already posted opportunities on my basic website, and that was without any marketing. Meanwhile, jobs in the milkround were falling away. It struck me that there was mileage in taking Enternships further.'

Others thought so too. A web development agency and a firm that ran graduate recruitment marketing for blue chips jointly contacted Dey, offering to build him a new version of the site and jazz up its branding, in exchange for a 40% stake in the site. 'I was naïve, new to the concept of equity, and pretty skint', Dey, now 25, remembers. He agreed to the deal.

Bootstrapping

Returning from university to his parents' home in Upminster, north east London, Dey unpacked his books and Blackberry and got to work. 'Enternships was self-funded – I'd agreed only sweat equity – so I lived the true bootstrapped lifestyle: at home with my parents, working out of my bedroom', he says. 'Not glamorous, but necessary to keep costs to a minimum.'

Dey's working day started at 8.30 a.m., when he sat at his bedroom desk to tackle an inbox full of enternship requests, technical problems and advertising requests from start-ups. 'Most days I'd then go into central London for meetings with firms and entrepreneurs, get home around 8 p.m. and be back at my desk doing follow-up work and emails again till around 11.30 p.m. The idea of work–life balance doesn't exist in start-up world.'

A few months in, Dey was already regretting his early strategy. 'I realised that the equity-swap I'd agreed was wrong', he says. 'Sweat equity was a bad decision – it meant that 40% of my business employment in the hands people who had their own business ventures to run, and weren't necessarily tied into the development of Enternships. I felt a bit stupid at having agreed to give away such a large chunk of the business – and thought I needed to change it if I was going to be able to make Enternships into a viable business.'

Buy back

After lengthy negotiations, Dey managed to use his savings to buy back 37.5% of the 40% stake he had sold, giving him control over 97.5% of Enternships. But he still didn't have the technical know-how to build the site. 'So I tried to commission another company to build a new version of the site. But they failed to deliver on their promise, wasting nine months plus loads of time and money.' As a result, Dey advises wannabe entrepreneurs to avoid outsourcing if possible. 'From my experience, I'd say try to either find a technical co-founder, or have enough money to hire a lead developer early on.'

By the time Enternships was ready for launch – using the basic site built by the original partner company – in May 2009, Dey had spent £10,000 on legal and development costs. To check the site worked before going live, he launched a beta version, inviting 100 start-ups he knew personally to set up company profiles and advertise roles, and asking some of his student friends to apply for positions. 'The only way I was able to do things on a shoestring budget was through help and support of people I knew, whether that was pro bono advice, securing sponsorship for a launch party, or just advice about raising investment and hiring people. Networking was essential', he says.

Enternships hosted 900 people at a launch party at the end of Global Entrepreneurship Week, with lastminute.com's Martha Lane Fox as keynote speaker. Press coverage the next day in the *Daily Telegraph* and on popular enterprise blogs like Springwise saw more than 300 start-ups pre-register as beta users. The economic environment – with high unemployment and a buzz around entrepreneurship – helped generate rampant interest amongst students, graduates and companies. Amongst the first firms to sign up were News International, publisher of *The Times* and the *Sun*, and Martha Lane Fox's karaoke venture Lucky Voice.

Dey says he felt fulfilled, 'doing something positive – helping people find jobs at a time of high unemployment, plus inspiring people to look at entrepreneurship as a career path'. His site was also generating considerable interest in the media and start-up community. But after 18 months of working for free and living at home, the entrepreneur needed Enternships to start making money.

New strategy

Dey realised one of his greatest successes had been in the marketing of Enternships. He had devoted a large chunk of the two years post-graduation that he'd spent working on the site on promotion, which he believes was crucial in his path to monetising the website. 'I found Twitter and Facebook to be great ways of generating new business leads', he says. 'If you become an "expert" in your space, the media come to you for your views. Being aware of relevant "hooks" and points of interest to the media and being prepared to provide case studies or statistics, and being proactive, all help in developing links to the press.'

Having done so, Dey had built Enternships into a brand that he believed to be strong enough to command charges. The market agreed. At the end of 2011, he introduced £80 listing fees, and began charging firms £125 for a premium listing for additional coverage. 'The fees were more expensive than [listing site] Gumtree but cheaper than [recruitment giant] Monster', says Dey. A second source of revenue sprung up when Enternship began charging for companies to be included in newsletter mailshots, and a third stream is about to arise as Dey is working on microsites for corporate partners. The first, Santander Bank, has signed up Enternships to create a platform for its small and medium-sized business customers to recruit interns.

As the first of his commercialisation ideas bedded in, Dey began seeking out his own funding and arranged meetings with angel investors – opting for them as opposed to VCs due to the latter's 'incessant focus on numbers'. It was, says Dey, 'time to organise more investment to fulfil the site's potential, particularly as I needed to bring developers on board.' The first thing he learnt was 'just how time-consuming the fundraising process can be'. He adds: 'It's important to meet with numerous investors, have legal and financial paperwork ready for due diligence and be prepared for follow-up meetings. Busy angels may not have the same time pressures as you.'

The process took Dey six months, but eventually he secured a six-figure sum from a portfolio of high-net-worth individuals. That allowed him to launch new features such as candidate profiling, industry specific landing pages for technology, fashion, PR and others, plus microsites, as well as hire a team of five including a full-time developer. More than 3000 businesses, including Groupon, Paypal, Wildfire Apps and pop star Lily Allen's retail store now use the site. It has more than 4000 advertised roles, and in excess of 150,000 page views, every month. 'Dealing with contracts, payroll, health and safety and the numerous other factors involved with hiring people was tough – a completely new experience', Dey says. But the site grew incrementally and, towards the end of 2011, he finally took a salary out of the business. Enternships has now finally moved out of Dey's bedroom into an office in London's burgeoning 'tech city' in Angel.

The future

Dey's ambition crosses seas and borders. 'Enternships has captured the imagination of so many people across the globe –

people have contacted me from Australia, India, China, South Africa, and the Middle East asking for a platform like this', he says. The site has 'soft launched' in South Africa and Dey and his team hope to develop similar microsites elsewhere. 'I want to be able to facilitate cross-border opportunities – given how global students are in nature and outlook, Enternships should be able to provide an opportunity for a UK student to do an Enternship in South Africa or a French student to do one in the UK.' He believes his likely exit will be a trade sale, 'either to a larger competitor or a media group', but for now his main priority is 'building a large and successful business'. And he is even able to afford to sign up his own enterns to help out.

Fact box: Enternships

Launch: 2009

Revenue: (forecast for 2012): £400,000

Staff: 5

Top tip: 'Find someone to share the burden of starting up if you can – it's a tough, but enjoyable, journey.'

Part Two: Advice

CHAPTER 12

THE LIGHTBULB MOMENT

'I'd love to be an entrepreneur', dreams Aye Wan Tobee Rich on yet another long commute into work. 'But I've never had that big idea that will make me the next Bill Gates.'

Struggling to isolate that elusive, amazing idea is one reason people cite for preventing them taking the leap to starting their own online business. The other? Not knowing how to go about it. They'll make reference to entrepreneurs like Richard Branson or Martha Lane Fox; super-successful people who've made millions from some brilliant ideas. But being an entrepreneur isn't easy – if it was, everyone would be doing it, rather than just talking about it. So the first idea to drag from desktop to recycling bin is the one about an amazing, unimprovable business concept popping into your brain one day, ready for launch seconds later.

Most of the world's most popular online ideas required honing to reach their potential. Think of Facebook. It started life as a way for Harvard students to check out potential girlfriends, then evolved and expanded to become the world's biggest social network. Likewise Google: Sergey Brin and Larry Page first created a simple search engine – originally called BackRub – whilst students at university. Now it's the biggest beast on the internet, taking in our homes (Maps, Streetview), email (Gmail), academia (Scholar), and videos (YouTube), with bigger ambitions emerging all the time. Very few businesses come from a bolt of perfectly formed inspiration: most will need you to refine, research and nurture.

The best thing a site can do is solve a problem. Think about it: Twitter disseminates information super-fast. Spotify makes music easily available anywhere. Amazon sells books cheaper than on the high street. A lot of online businesses originate from their founders spotting gaps in the market as a result of their own life experiences. Perhaps an annoying part of their job, hobby or daily routine, or a service that could be made quicker or easier if someone introduced an online shortcut. That's what triggered Zoopla founder Alex Chesterman to set up his property website: his own search for a new home saw him toiling over spreadsheets to work out house values in his potential new street, and he thought a website could do it for him. Millions of users now agree with him.

Likewise Made.com founder Ning Li: he wanted to buy a sofa, couldn't believe the high-street mark-up, so set up a site linking online shoppers direct to manufacturers. SpareRoom's founder Rupert Hunt started his site after failing to find a decent flat-share. He says life's little (or large) frustrations are the perfect source of business inspiration. 'If you're struggling to do something, the chances are everyone else is having the same problems', he says. 'If your product or service addresses an existing need, you'll stand a far better chance of success than if you try to create the need for whatever you're selling or copy another successful idea.'

Is there a specialist item that you wish was more available in the shops? If you think that, why wouldn't others? Online sales now account for close to a fifth of UK retail spending, and that's predicted to soar in the next few years. Or, if you haven't got any problems or shopping shortages that need solving yourself, talk to friends. Susan Holcome was a mother of four with no business or internet experience when she was at a dinner party listening to a friend moaning that he couldn't get a hat to fit his big head. She researched the problem, found it was a growing market as Britons were eating more and head sizes were increasing, and decided to start a big hat website. Holcolme ripped a few baseball hats apart, used the patterns to make prototypes, and ordered a thousand large hats and cycle helmets from China. It wasn't entirely straightforward – she was ripped off by her first Chinese manufacturer and ended up receiving 3000 not-quite-right hats that stocked south London's charity shops for months afterwards – but Max-cap.co.uk is now making Holcolme £10,000 a year, whilst she's working just an hour or two a day. One of the best things about the web is its accessibility. Not just for customers – though it does mean there are billions of potential users out there – but for start-ups.

Ideas can come from anywhere. Anthony Eskinazi dreamt up ParkatmyHouse.com in 2006 after inspiration struck on holiday in the US. 'I was making my way to a baseball stadium in San Francisco, and trying to get to the Giants' stadium, but finding a parking space was impossible', Eskinazi, who was 23 at the time, explains. 'Then I saw an empty driveway next door to the stadium, and realised that there was a great opportunity for both homeowners and drivers if only they could find a way of making the initial contact.' Four years later, Eskinazi's website has more than 30,000 parking spaces across the country and is earning its customers more than £1 million per year.

Certain markets have a bigger range of gaps to be filled, or particularly wallet-willing consumers. If you've just become a parent, congratulations: not just because little Phil or Lil is undoubtedly the most extraordinarily cute thing ever to grace planet Earth, but because you've just stumbled into a huge and booming online industry. Just think of sites like Kiddicare, the children's equipment website whose founders recently sold for £70 million to supermarket Morrison's, or Mumsnet, which makes its money by commoditising knowledge.

Networking with a wide range of people, particularly those doing a wildly different job from you, will also help you think up new ideas and stop getting stuck in a thought-rut.

Remember your idea doesn't have to be unique. If something already exists, you can create a copycat site: you just have to improve the existing offering, or bring it to a new market. Amazon wasn't the first online bookseller, but it's grown to be the biggest. Groupon wasn't the first group-buying site around – Wigadoo, for example, tried and failed a long time before – but it's the name to beat now. The first to market isn't always the first to make a mint, buy a yacht and move to Monte Carlo. Copycat ideas can work: just remember the advice of Groupon's Christopher Muhr, and work fast.

Whatever idea you settle on, work out your expectations before rushing in. Don't obsess over replicating the success of the big shots if all you want to do is create a sideline business to boost your income or solve a niche problem. Make it pay from the beginning – don't fall into the old argument about creating a great brand that you'll eventually sell for millions. Work out your monetisation strategy (see the next chapter) from the start. A busy little website that will help diversify your earnings is far more achievable as a first objective than creating that elusive 'new Facebook'.

Most importantly, be passionate. If you want to be a web entrepreneur, you're going to be the one who'll have to find the motivation to carry on at four in the morning, when your coding isn't going right or your Indian developer isn't getting your wish-list. Only an ongoing, aching hunger for your site's success will carry you through.

CHAPTER 13

THE IDEA: CHECKING IT OUT

Once you've conjured up a brilliant idea, don't keep it between you and the dog. The four-legged friend might be easy to impress, but he's not going to help you on the path to success. Sharing your idea might sound counterproductive, but it's crucial. Even in the earliest days of your business, you'll need to seek advice, try ideas, and test them out.

Market research

There's only one way to test your business idea out: ask people if they would use it. You need to ensure the market is big enough to fulfil your expectations. If you took your friend Bob – a vegetarian insomniac – as your inspiration to start up a live midnight forum discussing new meat-free recipes, check whether anyone else in the world would log in before plunging all your savings into the idea. It wouldn't take long to realise that it was ridiculous. But even if your idea is absolutely sane, you still need to establish whether there's a large enough market out there to foster success.

So, hunt for existing data from relevant trade press and online sources and – most importantly – talk to as many of your potential consumers as possible. Speak to people you know, and

more that you don't (they're more likely to be honest, and critical). What sites do they use now? Would they use the one you're
proposing? How often would they visit? What do they spend
their money on? How much would they spend on your site?
Who are they and how do they behave? What existing products
or services do they use? What marketing techniques are they
most likely to be swayed by? What site designs do they like?
Do they understand your idea – and would they use it?

Ask the simple questions – would they use your site or sign up
to buy your product or service at the price you're asking? If not,
why not? You could set up an online survey using a site like
Survey Monkey but, if possible, it's best to interview your
potential customers face-to-face. That means you could monitor
them online by seeing how they engage with rival sites. (Are
features tough to find, does it take too long to reach the checkout, is the security strong enough?) Later, once you start working
on your own site, you should keep engaging with these potential customers to gain feedback on your work. This is a crucial
part of creating a site via wireframing – making a bare-bones
site that you tweak and develop gradually and using user feedback, rather than spending months working on it before a 'big
reveal'. Find out more in Chapter 15, Creating a Website.

You also need to research competition in the market. Look for
feedback on the existing offering, plus pricing, usability, design,
and suppliers. You'll need all this background information to
work out your USP (will your service be faster, cheaper, more
comprehensive?) and, later on, to write a business plan.

Another group of people you need to speak to whilst checking
out your idea are potential investors: they're bound to puncture
your unbridled enthusiasm, but think of that as a good thing.
It's far easier to fix a problem early in the life cycle of an online
business than plough ahead, invest time and cash and then

discover your product or service already exists, or has other problems – giving a rival time to nip in, smooth out the offering and replicate your idea. Ask potential backers that you trust for their early thoughts on the idea, what they would like to see, what they would need in order to invest in the idea, and their preferred stage of investment. Again, there's more information on funding in Chapter 15, Setting up a Business.

Monetisation plan

'Tell all your readers not to do a Twitter!' exclaimed one big City venture capital investor when I told him about this book. Twitter might be a very popular website, with some 175 million users at last count, but analysts believe it has not yet worked out a revenue-raising strategy to fully capitalise on its scale. So work out how your website is going to make any money from its launch. Do you want it to be funded by advertising? If so, you should be aiming to draw in as many surfers as possible through entertainment or information. Are you keener on a site focused on sales and offering e-commerce – in which case your aim should be to retain surfers from homepage to receipt page. Do you want to create a spring-board-style, revenue-earning website which, like price-comparison services, will earn a commission for every sale your site bounces to other businesses? Or would you prefer a subscription-based model, requiring users to register and pay to use your site?

It's not just Twitter – a lot of big websites have become extraordinarily popular but struggle to earn revenues. If you're building a website to make money, working out how you're going to do so – and projecting growth and revenues from the start – will be crucial for your business plan, fundraising, marketing, site design – everything, really.

Barriers to entry

Your market research has established who your competitors are or what the marketplace is: next you need to ensure how you're going to take over the market or carve your own niche, and stop others from copying you. Be it building a strong brand or developing protected intellectual property like back-end algorithms, make sure you have thought about how your site will stay ahead of the competition – because the online marketplace is very easy to enter.

How much will it cost?

Before you sink all of your time and cash into an online start-up, make sure you can afford it. It's difficult to work out the cost of the actual site – it depends enormously on the scale of your ambition, the site's design and development and staff costs – but start making estimates early on to ensure you can afford it. If you're going to develop a site yourself, remember to factor in the value of your own time and the opportunity cost involved – all those hours you won't be spending earning money in a conventional job – and ensure you'll still be able to cover your living costs. Sainsbury's won't accept shares in your future start-up when you're at the checkout trying to pay for sausages with an empty wallet.

If you're going to outsource writing your site's code or design, or hire a full-time developer or other members of a founding team, go to suppliers to find out the market rate and calculate if you can afford to start up an online business.

Next, carry out thoroughly researched predictions of projected costs and revenues for the first few months, and then year one, two, three, four and five. Work out your margins and when you can expect to break even. It's best to carry out three projections – best, likely and worst-case scenarios – because there's little point creating a website that you can't afford to keep running.

Timing

Think about when you'll want to launch your site and how long it will take to establish. Little point making a big splash about your new site aimed at uni students in May when most will be buried in exams. If you're launching a specialist e-commerce site, think about particular events that could chime in. The e-tailer behind 'Crown Jewels Condoms' (crownjewels-condoms.com) for example – tagline: 'lie back and think of England' launched his products just before Prince William and Kate Middleton's Royal Wedding, creating a storm of interest on social networks and in the press to give a strong sales push.

You

Have you really thought about the reality of starting up an online business – and not just the sugar-coated, fast-forwarded version you see on *Dragons' Den*? Spend a few days at home, on your own, in front of your computer doing your research before committing yourself. Will you be able to stand working alone for weeks on end? Do you have the confidence to network and promote yourself and your business? Do you have the right numerical, technology, design or analytical tools – or the nous to find the best supplier or partner? Make sure you do before plunging ahead.

Solo or duet?

If your research has thrown up some skill-weakness areas, now could be the time to consider bringing a partner on board. If you're going to split ownership, you may as well share the hard work from the start. Securing a partner can also be a great way to solve the problem of a particular gap in your knowledge (like you're great with people but terrible with numbers) but you could equally just seek advice.

'There are plenty of people out there with ideas, it's the execution that really matters', says Rajeeb Dey of Enternships. For that, you'll need to find the right, talented people to join you in making your idea a reality: 'If you think you have the technical skills to create a successful venture, then go out and attend networking events, meet other entrepreneurs and start talking about ideas. Think about what the "pain points" in your industry are.'

It's also a good idea to network with other entrepreneurs to learn more about how they did it – the contacts are bound to be useful later on, when you're looking for anything from sources of funding to premises. There's a huge array of events for entrepreneurs in the UK, such as Open Coffee Club Meetups (meetup.com/opencoffee/) and those run by regional Chambers of Commerce. Many universities have enterprise societies and host external events.

'Talk to people who have launched a successful start-up company and grown it. Their advice will be invaluable to you', says Alex Buttle, co-founder of Top 10 Broadband, a price comparison site he started with friends in 2007. 'Speaking to business people who've been there, done that – especially in the web world – will help you be brave, but not stupid.' Buttle should know. He and his team built up Top 10 Broadband to a team of 18, generating revenues of over £10 million in 2010. He and his co-founders sold the business to bigger rival uSwitch.com in June 2011.

Do remember, however, to choose those you want to open up to cautiously – avoid your jealous ex-best friend looking for his own start-up idea; seek out your clever old school friend currently involved in online media – and be prepared to hear criticism. Carry out the research thoroughly but be quick too – if you've found a genuinely new web idea, getting it to market quickly could be key. And the next two chapters will help you do just that.

CHAPTER 14

SETTING UP A BUSINESS

It's not just a website you're creating, it's a business. Consequently, you'll have to sort out funding, write a business plan, set up and register as a UK company, organise tax affairs, recruitment, and become adroit at financial reporting. Depending on the size of your site and ambition, you might want to outsource your tax or accountancy work. But you'll still need to carefully consider which structure best suits your needs, and set up your company accordingly. Sole trader, limited liability company, or a partnership? The benefits and features of each are outlined here:

- *Sole trader*: this is the simplest of business structures, with a minimum of regulation. 'There's no obligation to file accounts publicly, but also no protection from creditors', says Patrick Harrison, partner at accountancy firm PKF. 'As a sole trader, you're personally responsible for any debts run up by your business, which could put your home or other assets at risk.' Tax is charged according to the business's profits as declared in your personal tax return, and is not affected by the amount of money that may be withdrawn from the business.

- *Limited liability company*: here the company's finances are separate from the director's (or directors') personal finances, as distinct from a sole trader. Shareholders are not liable for any debts run up by the business, except if directors guarantee loans or credit taken out in the company's name. Limited liability companies must have at least one member and at least one director, and be registered at Companies House. Accounts have to be prepared annually in accordance with standard accounting principles and must, in many cases, be professionally audited.

Since the company and its shareholders are also separate legal entities, the company can take – and be the subject of – legal action in its own name. The company will be liable to corporation tax on profits (see below). 'To extract profits from a company, payments will generally be made by way of salary or dividend', says Harrison. 'Where the company is owned by the manager(s), they will be able to choose how and when this is done and take advantage of the different regimes applying for tax and National Insurance contributions.

'But it's important to remember that funds in the company's accounts belong to the company, not its owners, until a salary or dividend payments are made. Generally, any payment of cash into the hands of an owner will result in a tax liability arising either on the company or the recipient. Entrepreneurs can easily get into difficulties if they treat their companies' accounts as their own – this can trigger unexpected tax liabilities.' In this kind of business structure, entrepreneurs must file an annual return giving details of the company's officers and shareholders and details of any transfers of shares since the last annual return date.

- *Partnership*: the ownership of the business is shared by two or more people outside a limited company. 'Profits are shared among partners, and each is personally responsible for paying tax on their share of the profits, and for National Insurance contributions', says Harrison. 'Each must register for Self Assessment with HMRC and complete an annual tax return, whilst one (nominated) partner must also send the taxman a partnership return.'

- *Limited Liability Partnership (LLP)*: these have to meet similar financial disclosure and statutory filing requirements to UK companies, including filing an annual return and accounts. An LLP is a separate legal entity from its owners, and offers protection in the same way as a limited company, but for tax purposes is still treated in the same way as a general partnership.

Comparison of the main business vehicles

	Limited company	Sole trader	General partnership	LLP
Creditor protection	yes	no	no	yes
Public filing	yes	no	no	yes
Personal tax on profits	no	yes	yes	yes
Personal tax on funds withdrawn	yes	no	no	no
Appropriate for external investors	yes	no	no	yes
Easy to convert to a different vehicle	no	yes	yes	no
Easy to withdraw funds	no	yes	yes	yes
Easy to close down	no	yes	no	no

Business plan

Whatever source of funding you're organising (see below for the options), unless your site is a bootstrap (self-funded) project, you'll need to create a business plan to bring backers on board.

Any banks, external investors, grant or loan organisations, potential partners and possible buyers will all want to see it, so remember it's an organic document that you should update and amend as your business develops. You'll also need to tailor your plan for your audience – many banks, for example, have interactive services helping those seeking a start-up loan to include the details they need. As a general rule, however, business plans should include:

- *An executive summary.* This provides an overview of your online business. Think of it as your elevator pitch – many investors will use this opening statement to form their judgement about your business. Keep this section to a maximum of two pages long; avoid hyperbole and fluffy language, but equally don't be too curt or overambitious. Be realistic, passionate, honest and straight.

- *A description of the business's goals and opportunities available.* This is the who, what and why of the site: the market it will fill, what you plan to sell or offer, why and to what audience, and why your site will be disruptive or different to existing products or services. List your legal structure, the site's unique selling points, whether you hold any patents or other intellectual property, and your development plans. Avoid insider jargon: a banker reading your business plan may know little about the online world, for example.

- *Information about you, the founding team and, if applicable, advisory board.* This should include your professional history and skills, what makes you the ideal founding team to run the site, and CVs of key personnel. Lenders examining a business plan will want to see evidence of security you're prepared to use as insurance against anything going wrong in the business, so prepare detail on your assets.

- *Marketing and sales strategy.* Who are your customers and how will you woo them? How will you create higher barriers to entry to prevent others taking your market, either through intellectual property, marketing or branding? Detail your sales and revenue strategy, and information about the competition (if applicable) and why your idea/business is different.

- *Information on your operations.* Where is your work space, what are its facilities, what equipment and IT infrastructure are you using? What are your current and expected staff numbers?

- *Financial forecasts.* This should include the money you require, what you'll do with it and how you'll use it to help the site grow. List all previous funding, and where it's from; include the key risks to the business, such as competitor action, IT failure, a break-up of the management team or acts of God, and detail how those problems will be overcome. Include a sales and cash flow forecast for five years, as well as projected profit and loss figures.

Overall, keep the business plan tight but include enough information to explain your company and its ambitions. Line up at least three people (one outside of your industry, one insider, one financial expert such as an accountant) to proof-check it, and ensure all figures, statements and projections are both realistic and accurate. Add any extra documents such as market research in appendices at the back, rather than clogging up your text.

Financial reporting and accounting

It might not be as fun as site design or as exciting as launch day, but UK law requires every company (and LLP) to keep proper accounting records and prepare accounts for every financial year to be filed at Companies House. For these, you must keep records of all receipts and payments and all sales and purchases of goods for at least six years. Although sole proprietors aren't legally compelled to keep accounting records in the same way, they must still maintain records to support their tax return.

'HMRC now carries out live Business Records Checks and will expect a business's records for the current year to be up to date', warns Harrison at PKF. 'Businesses that fail to do this will be reprimanded and repeat offenders may face a tax penalty or find their business subject to a time consuming and intrusive tax investigation.'

Most tax administration can now be done online, and Business Link and the taxman have developed a tool to help start-ups work out the records needing to be retained here: http://tinyurl. com/bizlinktax.

Tax

As an entrepreneur, these are the taxes you're most likely to incur:

- *Income tax*. Charged on total income in each tax year, running from 6 April to 5 April. Calculated by adding up all income, then subtracting relevant tax allowances and reliefs, and applying the appropriate rates. 'Self-employed individuals (or members of a partnership) must notify HMRC when they start trading, and pay tax on their trading profits in a tax year', says Harrison. 'But entrepreneurs can choose an accounting period that suits the business best – this need not be the same as the tax year.

In the early years, careful choice of the accounting date can considerably help with cash flow. Any losses made, for example, can be claimed against other income to reduce the total tax liability for the year. Excess losses can be carried forward to reduce taxable profit in future years, and losses can be carried back in the early years of trade, if beneficial.'

Income tax is paid on account – in advance – in two chunks, one on 31 January in the tax year and one on 31 July, both based on 50% of the prior year's liability. Any balance, together with any capital gains tax which may be due, is payable with the submission of the personal tax return online by 31 January following the end of the tax year. If you submit a paper return, the deadline is 31 October, and penalties are charged if you are late submitting it. Depending when you start a business, it can be some time before the first payment is due and you should budget to ensure that funds are available when needed.

- *Corporation tax.* Levied on the taxable, worldwide profits of UK resident companies, based on its annual accounts. Normally payable nine months and one day after the end of the period for which a company prepares its accounts. 'Again, trading losses for one accounting period can be used to reduce taxable profits for other periods', says Harrison. A UK company must normally submit a tax return within 12 months of its accounting year end. The UK corporation tax year runs from 1 April to 31 March. The top rate of corporation tax for the year to 31 March 2012 is 26%. A small company tax rate of 20% applies for the year to 31 March 2012. The top rate of tax is currently charged on the whole of a company's taxable profit if it reaches £1.5 million.

- *National insurance contributions.* Payable by employers, employees and self-employed people. If your start-up employs staff, either permanently or on a temporary basis, you'll have to deduct NIC from the salary paid and pay it to HMRC. 'Even if no formal employment contract exists, if an individual works exclusively for another individual, a partnership or a company on a regular basis, this is likely to constitute employment and the employer should deduct both NIC and income tax from the amounts paid to the individual', says Harrison.

  For the tax year to 5 April 2012, where an individual's gross earnings exceed £602 per month, Class 1 NIC must be deducted from the individual's salary at a rate of 12% until monthly earnings reach £3,541, from which point a rate of 2% applies. Employers must also pay NIC at 13.8% on the total salary in excess of £589 per month paid to the individual. NIC must also be paid on the value of non-salary benefits, like private medical insurance.

  Self-employed people are liable for Class 2 NIC (£2.50 per week) as well as Class 4 NIC paid at 9% profits between £7,225 and £42,475 per annum and 2% on any excess.

- *PAYE.* If you employ staff, you must register as an employer with HMRC and deduct pay-as-you-earn tax as well as NIC from salary payments.

- *Value added tax.* If your sales are likely to exceed the annual threshold (£73,000 for the year beginning 1 April 2011), you must become VAT-registered. VAT is a sales tax charged on the supply of goods and services provided in the course of doing business in the UK. The burden for paying normally falls on the consumer, with the intervening businesses acting as collecting agents for the government. The standard rate of VAT is 20%, but education, finance, health and insurance are exempt from this tax. It's important also to consider the impact of VAT on your customers. If they are businesses, they may be able to claim back the tax you charge them but individual consumers will not.

- *Business rates.* Based on the value of the property's land and buildings, set by central government.

Funding

A small site may be easy to set up in your spare time with just a hundred pounds at launch; a big one could cost millions. Your best source of funding will depend on the size of your business and ambition, and thus the level of funding required. First things first: what are your options?

1. Bootstrapping – funding the project yourself, perhaps through a bank overdraft, or working at the same time.
2. Equity finance – swapping a stake in the business for cash. You might raise the money from friends and family, angel investors, or a venture capital fund.
3. Debt funding – taking out a loan.

1. Bootstrapping
A popular option for small start-ups, who can create a site whilst working or consulting, or using savings, then later fund it using customer revenues. This method will ensure you're very cost-conscious and lean – and ramp up the urgency of generating revenues. But it could also limit your growth and pace of development.

2. Equity finance

Unlike debt funding, an injection of equity funding means not needing to worry about paying funds back in the short or medium terms – or shelling out interest payments. Investors will pay cash in return for ownership of a stake of your site. They will usually demand a significant return for their risk and, since they won't get their money back unless the site is sold or through dividends funded by growth, they will usually only be interested in involvement if your business plan shows a growth rate of at least 15% per year. Equity finance may also provide strategic opportunities or useful advice for your business, which can provide huge value. The main sources of equity finance are as follows.

Friends, former work colleagues and family

Those who know your proven ability may be more willing to back your website idea and execution of it. If you do go down this route, however, don't keep it casual: make sure you write up a shareholder agreement to avoid any arguments later down the line. Typical agreements should cover what happens if one of the shareholders dies, files for bankruptcy, resigns, retires, is fired or unable to work; the value of shares; whether the company will be forced to buy back stock of a departing share-holder, and how much would be paid for that stock.

Business angels

Wealthy individuals known as business angels are often former (or current) entrepreneurs. They tend to provide sums above £25,000 but below £250,000 to invest in new businesses. For that, angel investors are likely to ask for at least 10% of the business, or significantly more for an early-stage start-up. 'The level of involvement in the day-to-day running of the business expected by angel investors will vary', says Stephen Bayfield, partner specialising in fundraising at accountancy firm PKF. 'Some seek no day-to-day involvement whatsoever, while others are keen to secure involvement within the business and add value to their investment with their experience.'

The best way to access a business angel is through networking, but there are also established introduction services that match potential investors with businesses seeking finance, such as the Angel Investment Network and Venture Giant (see resources chapter). It's useful to note that angels are also a key part of the ecosystem of venture capital, meaning they can be a natural route into the VC world for larger pools of funding if that's required at a later stage of your site's development.

Private equity

If your website demands larger investment, then private equity houses, venture capitalists (VCs) or family offices (funds managed on behalf of wealthy individuals or families) may be the best option. Few VCs consider investing in early-stage businesses (and will typically demand a compound return in excess of 30%) so if that's your requirement, you'll have to stand out. 'VCs will require evidence of a sound management track record, a robust business proposition and a clear exit plan', says Bayfield. 'In return, they may provide not only financial support but also, if they specialise in the business sector concerned, valuable relevant experience and contacts that will assist in developing the business growth.'

Alex Chesterman at Zoopla took the VC funding path because he knew he would need more money in the future. 'VCs generally have more appetite and ability to provide further funds as the business progresses. Entrepreneurs raising funds have to balance dilution via funding with the upside potential which is why it is preferable to raise funds in multiple rounds at increasing valuations providing the business is operating successfully.'

Errol Damelin also funded his money lending site Wonga via several rounds of VC funding, but warns that it's only appropriate 'in very narrow circumstances – those where you're creating something truly disruptive requiring a lot of capital, and where there's a meaningful probability that your idea is so good it will blow the competition out of the water.' He adds, 'If your site can't use multiple millions of pounds productively, and turn that it into thirty times that amount you've raised, there's no point approaching a VC.'

If you believe your site can, however, then the first obstacle to wooing a VC will be getting through the door. Most established funds receive around 3500 approaches a year. They'll invite around 900 of those to send in a business plan, meet about 200 of those, and engage in several meetings with 50, before actually opting to invest in as few as 12 per year. So you need to get noticed. Many of the start-ups who receive funds from a VC have members of their founding team who have worked with the moneymen before: if you haven't, try to seek out an angel investor to get you an introduction. Most VCs won't appreciate being cold-called. 'The only way to do it is to get a recommendation', says Damelin. 'You have to network and get hold of people who VCs want to listen to, and then get them to recommend you.' If you're short of contacts, attend entrepreneurial meet-ups like Seedcamp, Springboard in Cambridge and other networking events – see the list of useful links at the end of this book for others.

Most VCs prefer to invest in businesses with a team and revenue model in place. 'The biggest thing to avoid', says Alan Wallace of VC Octopus Ventures, who has invested in Lovefilm, Zoopla and software company Prismastar, 'is high expectations of what the business is worth. Be realistic about both your ambitions and how much money you need. If you have huge expectations of growth and ask for loads of money, you need a basis for those expectations. Likewise, if you're not asking for a reasonable amount of money, a VC deal won't work.'

Wallace says the major features VCs look for in a business plan are:

- a team with a proven ability to deliver – be it in another start-up or a managerial role;
- a market niche; and
- a strong product.

You need to stress what's special about your business, and show that you've thought about building barriers to entry, whether through intellectual property or via thoughtful branding.

Before any meetings, prepare by researching the investors you're about to engage with, and know, in detail, about the deals that they have done in the past. More important than that, however, is knowing your own business, its projections and growth plans in huge detail. Make sure your business plan is thoroughly considered, including a clear revenue strategy, a clean set of legal contracts, and an investment plan that would leave a large enough option pool to share out amongst a future management team.

Prove how your business will achieve your growth projects, in detail. Use analytics, for example, to demonstrate that for every £1 spent, you'll get, say, 20 new users or customers, with 10 falling out and 10 providing lasting value. That shows VCs how cost-effective the site will be in getting customers and retaining them, and how their investment would generate growth. 'You'll need metrics to substantiate growth, not just big claims', says Wallace.

'Any investment needs two core ingredients – a really interesting market opportunity and a management team of sufficiently high calibre to take advantage of it', adds Patrick Reeve, managing partner at VC Albion Ventures, whose portfolio includes Lowcosttravelgroup.com and MiPay. 'Questions I ask include: is the opportunity in a growth market? Is it sufficiently differentiated? Does it have decent barriers to entry, or can someone else copy and get in easily? Has anyone in the management team run their own business before? In a relevant sector? Was it successful? If the answers to all these is "yes", then it's certainly worth us having a look.'

You'll have to put your trust in the VC directors – most don't appreciate non-disclosure agreements. 'I've never bought into a business demanding an NDA', Wallace adds. 'If someone wants to talk to me about their business but they don't trust me, it doesn't bode well.' Once you're through the door, Wallace advises it's crucial to present your case 'in a very positive way. The people who get money from us need to be exceptional individuals – highly motivated by financial achievement, with fantastic energy and a totally disruptive idea. Online, the barriers to entry are very low and copycats can quickly follow a good idea, so it comes down to execution of an idea – can you and your the team deliver well, have you set yourselves achievable targets and can you prove you've already made and are still making progress? That's what we want to know in that first meeting. We're not a bank, we don't take collateral, so we're lending against the management team and its ability to change markets and create businesses.'

If you've wooed a VC and are thrashing out a deal, don't congratulate yourself at your success: stay savvy. Avoid giving away anti-dilution rights, and be wary about VCs who want too much control, such as the exclusive right to appoint a chairman: those kind of responsibilities should be shared.

What you should expect VCs to do, however, is demand emails once a month detailing progress, ask for attendance at board meetings and remuneration committees, and perhaps also have a role in any committee selecting new team members. They'll often also want to see a set of accounts once a month.

Most VCs will insist on a three-month maximum notice period, even for the founder. 'There's no reward for failure in the entrepreneurial world', says Wallace. VCs are also likely to insist on salaries no higher than between £50,000 and £70,000 for the founding team, with a strong emphasis on bonus and performance-related targets. You can – and should – argue about terms, but it's not a good idea to get involved in final-stage negotiations with more than one VC at the same time. 'It's not *Dragons' Den* – Britain's entrepreneurial community is small', says Wallace, 'and if someone's playing me off against other VCs to push up my price I'll walk away immediately.'

Venture capital alternatives

With few VCs now investing less than £1 million, the 'equity gap' – the cavity between funds that can be raised through friends and family and angel investors and the much higher starting point for most venture capitals – is partly being addressed by Enterprise Capital Funds. This government-backed initiative can yield investments of up to £2 million on a matched funding basis. The schemes are run by Capital for Enterprise Limited – www.capitalforenterprise.gov.uk. Other linked, or similar government-backed funds include Aspire, a £12.5 million risk capital fund which invests in businesses led by women, the UK Innovation Investment Fund, and Nesta's innovation investment pool.

3. Debt funding

Financing your business via debt allows growth without you diluting your ownership or losing control of running the company. You will know all the costs in advance, which helps cash flow, but will also have to repay the debt within a defined period. 'In considering how much debt a business takes on, think about the servicing costs and repayment profile, and ensure this can be comfortably met from your business's projected cash flow', advises Bayfield. 'Debt demands a lower return than equity – but the return will be closely linked to the security, the size of the company and strength of future cash flows.'

Overdraft

Borrowing money from a bank via an overdraft is one of the easiest sources of cash, but institutions can call in the money at short notice. 'Its use should generally be restricted to short-term cash-flow funding, with longer term needs met by more structured loans', advises Bayfield.

Other loans are also available from sources including the Enterprise Finance Guarantee Scheme, where the government guarantees up to 75% of a loan. It's open to businesses with an annual turnover of up to £25 million, seeking finance of £1000 to £1 million, repayable over a period of between three months and ten years. Other loans include hire purchase to buy items like expensive technology, and the Community Development Finance Initiative, which provides loans and support to businesses in particular areas (www.cdfa.org.uk).

Recruitment

As an online start up, when you're ready to start hiring staff, you'll have to tackle all the usual issues – anti-discrimination law, interviewing, disciplinary problems, and creating a work-place policy – but may have another, unusual set of problems on top of those. You might not be able to afford a market-rate salary, for example, even though your site is almost certain to demand gruesome hours from its staff, at least at first when the business gets off the ground.

Plus, your start-up will be just that – not a big brand able to lure the best thanks to its cool cachet, but an unknown entity that could struggle to recruit the best. The answer, according to Karl Gregory, who runs the dating site match.com in Britain, is to 'identify your key people and give them equity'. Don't, he adds, be scared of diluting your stake. 'It's crucial to create passion and loyalty.'

Gregory's career spanned techy corporates like Yahoo and start-ups, including local business directory site TouchLocal.com. But when he started running Match, he had to work out some recruitment rules for the internet world. 'The most important hire most online entrepreneurs make is their first one', he says. 'Any early stage cycle business needs a developer and someone with commercial acumen. Some people have both. Most start-ups will look for the other skill in a founding partner. As the business grows, online entrepreneurs need to continuously work out the skills you're missing and seek them out. Great founding teams are often very creative, and chasing lots of ideas at the same time. But older companies need to be more focused with a clear communications drive.'

Don't be scared of hiring people who you think are better than you. 'They'll push you to work harder', says Gregory. But never get involved in a bidding war: future staff should be passionate about wanting to work for your company. 'Don't accept second best when recruiting', says Errol Damelin, of Wonga. 'Virtually everyone who joined our site took a big pay cut. We couldn't afford the market rate, but we offered an equity share and reverted to market rate when we could afford it. If someone won't accept that, then they don't believe in the idea and may not be the right person.'

Once your hires are in place, it's crucial to develop a strong team culture. As a start-up, you might not have the cash that a big corporate has to flash around, but you will be nimble and know your team far more closely, so make the most of it. 'Don't just talk hot air, hold staff events and work with a charity that matches your ideals', says Gregory. 'The ethos at Match is to grow our staff across their professional or personal skills. For example we have a member of staff who teaches yoga in her spare time, a massage therapist, and a wedding first dance instructor who all hold sessions at the office to hone their skills. We also work with a charity that mentors teenagers.'

Premises or working from home

A lot of small-scale online start-ups launch from their founder's home, but if you go down this route, be aware that the decision could impact your tax, mortgage and insurance payments. Some mortgages, for example, don't allow a home to be used as a workplace, whilst doing so could invalidate some home insurance policies. Check this out before going ahead. On the plus side, working from home could mean your business can claim tax relief on utility bills for the parts of the house used for your work. It could also, however, see you charged business tax rates rather than council tax – on which, more below.

If you choose to rent or buy your own premises, you'll almost certainly have to pay business rates. The Valuation Office Agency will give your office a rateable value, and your local authority will then calculate how much you should pay in rates.

The government advisory service Business Link has an online calculator to work out approximate rates. http://tinyurl.com/bizlinkcalculator.

Intellectual property

Every online start-up will have some kind of IP – intellectual property – whether it's an algorithm, branding, invention, software, design or other kind of creative work. You need to think about protecting the work you have created – as well as avoiding infringing the rights of other companies.

Most digital assets – like photos or software – are automatically protected by copyright laws, which cover anything that is recorded or written down, meaning there's no need to register ownership. If work is created by an employee, the copyright owner will usually be the employer, but an independent contractor (say a web designer) will own the copyright to their work unless the contract commissioning the work includes a clause requiring copyright to be transferred.

Likewise, if you want to use someone else's digital assets on your site, you need to seek permission from the owner of the copyright. But there are a wide range of other areas of IP law, from patents (which protect inventions, which could include the back-end features of a website), designs, and trademarks for logos or brand names. IP is complicated and you'll often need professional advice from a patent or trademark attorney. The UK's Intellectual Property Office also offers a free IP Healthcheck tool online, covering trademarks, designs, patents and copyright, with realms of advice to help you both protect and exploit your IP rights. It holds free IP awareness seminars around the country and lists advisors to help you find out more. www.ipo.gov.uk.

Internet usage policies

Another area of law you need to consider is a set of internet legal policies, setting out, for example, what you will do with users' personal data, and copyright of site content.

The advisory service Business Link offers a set of sample legal documents which can be used without copyright infringement. Its terms and conditions template for website usage reads:

> *Welcome to our website. If you continue to browse and use this website, you are agreeing to comply with and be bound by the following terms and conditions of use, which together with our privacy policy govern [business name]'s relationship with you in relation to this website. If you disagree with any part of these terms and conditions, please do not use our website.*
>
> *The term '[business name]' or 'us' or 'we' refers to the owner of the website whose registered office is [address]. Our company registration number is [company registration number and place of registration]. The term 'you' refers to the user or viewer of our website.*
>
> *The use of this website is subject to the following terms of use:*
>
> - *The content of the pages of this website is for your general information and use only. It is subject to change without notice.*
>
> - *This website uses cookies to monitor browsing preferences. If you do allow cookies to be used, the following personal information may be stored by us for use by third parties: [insert list of information].*
>
> - *Neither we nor any third parties provide any warranty or guarantee as to the accuracy, timeliness, performance, completeness or suitability of the information and materials found or offered on this website for any particular purpose. You acknowledge that such*

information and materials may contain inaccuracies or errors and we expressly exclude liability for any such inaccuracies or errors to the fullest extent permitted by law.

- *Your use of any information or materials on this website is entirely at your own risk, for which we shall not be liable. It shall be your own responsibility to ensure that any products, services or information available through this website meet your specific requirements.*

- *This website contains material which is owned by or licensed to us. This material includes, but is not limited to, the design, layout, look, appearance and graphics. Reproduction is prohibited other than in accordance with the copyright notice, which forms part of these terms and conditions.*

- *All trademarks reproduced in this website which are not the property of, or licensed to, the operator are acknowledged on the website.*

- *Unauthorised use of this website may give rise to a claim for damages and/or be a criminal offence.*

- *From time to time this website may also include links to other websites. These links are provided for your convenience to provide further information. They do not signify that we endorse the website(s). We have no responsibility for the content of the linked website(s).*

- *Your use of this website and any dispute arising out of such use of the website is subject to the laws of England, Northern Ireland, Scotland and Wales.*

You should also list a privacy policy, which describes what information you will ask users for, what you will do with it, and how you will keep it secure. Business Link's template for an online privacy policy reads:

This privacy policy sets out how [business name] uses and protects any information that you give [business name] when you use this website.

[business name] is committed to ensuring that your privacy is protected. Should we ask you to provide certain information by which you can be identified when using this website, then you can be assured that it will only be used in accordance with this privacy statement.

[business name] may change this policy from time to time by updating this page. You should check this page from time to time to ensure that you are happy with any changes. This policy is effective from [date].

We may collect the following information:

- *name and job title*
- *contact information including email address*
- *demographic information such as postcode, preferences and interests*
- *other information relevant to customer surveys and/or offers*

What we do with the information we gather

We require this information to understand your needs and provide you with a better service, and in particular for the following reasons:

- *Internal record keeping.*
- *We may use the information to improve our products and services.*
- *We may periodically send promotional emails about new products, special offers or other information which we think you may find interesting using the email address which you have provided.*
- *From time to time, we may also use your information to contact you for market research purposes. We may contact you by email, phone, fax or mail. We may use*

the information to customise the website according to your interests.

Security

We are committed to ensuring that your information is secure. In order to prevent unauthorised access or disclosure, we have put in place suitable physical, electronic and managerial procedures to safeguard and secure the information we collect online.

How we use cookies

A cookie is a small file which asks permission to be placed on your computer's hard drive. Once you agree, the file is added and the cookie helps analyse web traffic or lets you know when you visit a particular site. Cookies allow web applications to respond to you as an individual. The web application can tailor its operations to your needs, likes and dislikes by gathering and remembering information about your preferences.

We use traffic log cookies to identify which pages are being used. This helps us analyse data about webpage traffic and improve our website in order to tailor it to customer needs. We only use this information for statistical analysis purposes and then the data is removed from the system.

Overall, cookies help us provide you with a better website by enabling us to monitor which pages you find useful and which you do not. A cookie in no way gives us access to your computer or any information about you, other than the data you choose to share with us.

You can choose to accept or decline cookies. Most web browsers automatically accept cookies, but you can usually modify your browser setting to decline cookies if you prefer. This may prevent you from taking full advantage of the website.

Links to other websites

Our website may contain links to other websites of interest. However, once you have used these links to leave our site, you should note that we do not have any control over that other website. Therefore, we cannot be responsible for the protec-

tion and privacy of any information which you provide whilst visiting such sites and such sites are not governed by this privacy statement. You should exercise caution and look at the privacy statement applicable to the website in question.

Controlling your personal information

You may choose to restrict the collection or use of your personal information in the following ways:

- *whenever you are asked to fill in a form on the website, look for the box that you can click to indicate that you do not want the information to be used by anybody for direct marketing purposes*

- *if you have previously agreed to us using your personal information for direct marketing purposes, you may change your mind at any time by writing to or emailing us at [email address]*

We will not sell, distribute or lease your personal information to third parties unless we have your permission or are required by law to do so. We may use your personal information to send you promotional information about third parties which we think you may find interesting if you tell us that you wish this to happen.

You may request details of personal information which we hold about you under the Data Protection Act 1998. A small fee will be payable. If you would like a copy of the information held on you please write to [address].

If you believe that any information we are holding on you is incorrect or incomplete, please write to or email us as soon as possible at the above address. We will promptly correct any information found to be incorrect.

You should also consider a website disclaimer which sets out the limitations of your liability for the use of your website and the information it contains. Business Link's sample disclaim reads:

The information contained in this website is for general information purposes only. The Information is provided by [business name] and while we endeavour to keep the information up to date and correct, we make no representations or warranties of any kind, express or implied, about the completeness, accuracy, reliability, suitability or availability with respect to the website or the information, products, services, or related graphics contained on the website for any purpose. Any reliance you place on such information is therefore strictly at your own risk.

In no event will we be liable for any loss or damage including without limitation, indirect or consequential loss or damage, or any loss or damage whatsoever arising from loss of data or profits arising out of, or in connection with, the use of this website.

Through this website you are able to link to other websites which are not under the control of [business name]. We have no control over the nature, content and availability of those sites. The inclusion of any links does not necessarily imply a recommendation or endorse the views expressed within them.

Every effort is made to keep the website up and running smoothly. However, [business name] takes no responsibility for, and will not be liable for, the website being temporarily unavailable due to technical issues beyond our control.

Lastly, you should also set out an internet copyright notice to tell users whether or not you will allow your material to be downloaded or distributed by others. Business Link's suggested text is as follows:

This website and its content is copyright of [business name] – © [business name] [year]. All rights reserved.

Any redistribution or reproduction of part or all of the contents in any form is prohibited other than the following:

  - *you may print or download to a local hard disk extracts for your personal and non-commercial use only*

- *you may copy the content to individual third parties for their personal use, but only if you acknowledge the website as the source of the material*

You may not, except with our express written permission, distribute or commercially exploit the content. Nor may you transmit it or store it in any other website or other form of electronic retrieval system.

Banking

You never know when you will need to turn to your bank in times of need so, even if you don't plan to apply for an overdraft or ask your bank for any funding or business help, it's always worth developing a good relationship with your bank to ensure they understand your business and what you're looking to achieve.

If you are intending to approach banks for funding, however, your business plan will be key. Getting good PR coverage and securing a couple of good clients can help give a bank some confidence if they're deciding whether to offer you a financing facility. But realism is the most important part of a successful business plan, according to the business banking experts at NatWest who receive thousands of proposals each year. 'Set yourself realistic objectives', advises a spokesman for the high-street bank. 'Make sure you have researched the financial side of the business fully, research your market and determine what you need to achieve your aims. Think carefully about the resources needed to make your plan work – premises, equipment, raw materials, machinery, labour. When presenting your case, you are selling the project and the banker is the customer. Make sure you know the facts and figures. Most of all understand your business plan and then monitor progress through it so you can exploit success and limit problems. Be open and realistic with all the facts. That way you will have a solid base for the banking relationship you will need in the future.'

If you struggle with cash later in the lifespan of your business, it will be far easier to organise a swift overdraft if you've already met your branch's business banking manager and shown him or her your business plan. To avoid that situation, though, it's crucial to think about cash flow from the beginning. The reason most businesses fail is because they run out of cash to pay the bills. Organise a buffer so that if it takes time for revenues to start coming in, or if customers or advertisers do not pay on time, you'll still be able to pay for your costs. According to the small business team at Royal Bank of Scotland, the best ways for start-ups to keep afloat in the tough early stage include:

- When issuing larger invoices, consider requesting stage payments or even cash on delivery to limit your risk of bad debts.
- Set your terms of business before doing business – and put them in writing. You will not be paid in 30 days unless customers know that's what you expect.
- Carry our credit checks before doing business – and monitor late payments. If companies are taking longer and longer to pay, find out if there is a problem. Don't wait until they leave you with a bad debt.
- Encourage prompt payment. Consider charging interest on late payments (your legal right on debts outstanding after 30 days) or – if your profit margins allow it – offering a discount for prompt payment.
- Invoice promptly, making payment terms clear.

- Make it easy for customers to pay you by offering as many ways of getting paid as you can. BACS payments are fast and attract lower bank charges. Or a standing order can be used if they pay the same amount regularly. With cheques your late payers can always use the excuse 'it's in the post'.

- Contact customers to check they received the invoice and then find out when they are going to pay – phone on day 40 to check you will be paid on day 60.

- Have a system in place to monitor cash flow: 8 in 10 businesses say they are currently seeing an increase in the number of their customers paying late.

- Monitor your website's financial health, keeping track of key figures like daily unique hits, conversions (surfers who click on advertising, proceed to e-commerce check out, etc.), stock, costs and late payment.

- Shave costs down to the quick but remember some things just shouldn't be cut. Don't scrimp on the staff expertise you need, sales, site development and marketing to build your business and, if relevant, insurance.

CHAPTER 15

CREATING A WEBSITE

Setting up a website involves some basic components which can then grow exponentially depending on the size and scale of your ambition. Every site needs a domain, server space and design. From there, many online entrepreneurs will want to hire a developer. This chapter outlines both the DIY site-making options and the intricacies of the techy route: professional developers divulge what exactly you should ask and demand before signing a contract. On design, a user experience expert outlines what you should look out for, and objectives to work towards. Plus, an online entrepreneur who has suffered the stings of troublesome outsourcing before getting it right reveals his learnt-from-experience tips for success.

The domain name

This is your shop front, the name above your door, and the first opportunity you have to encourage people to come on in. It's the first sign of your brand and your business. So make sure it's a good one.

Unfortunately, that won't be as easy as it was a decade ago. Not only are there now millions of sites already up and running, but an entire industry has also built up around buying and selling domain names – the highest price ever paid for a single domain was $13 million – for sex.com – in 2010. A blight of 'cyber squatters' who creep onto unused domains and hang around until someone offers them enough cash to move on has also sprung up.

The options

There are three types of domain name: generic Top Level Domains (gTLDs) which are not associated with any country, like *.com*, *.net*, *.edu*, *.gov* and *.org*. Then country domain names, like *.co.uk* in the UK, or *.ru* in Russia. Within those, there are second level domain names including *.org.uk*, and *.ltd.uk* for registered company names. Choose which type of domain you want – a small or UK-orientated start-up might be happy with .co.uk., one with international ambitions may want a gTLD like .com. It's often worth buying a few domains to stop rivals purchasing your name and encroaching on your territory, as well as to aid possible overseas expansion later on.

Next steps

Brainstorm some domain name ideas. Remember you're limited to alphanumeric characters plus hyphens only. Make a list of names, using the guidelines below, before moving on to the next phase: checking availability.

Tips

Make it as easy as possible for surfers to find your site. Avoid numerical substitutions – 4 instead of 'for' may be confusing when a site is being discussed aloud, for example. Avoid zero as it could be viewed as the letter 'o'. Pick words with only one possible spelling.

Hyphens can make a URL cheaper. But be wary: they're easily forgettable, and people may struggle to find your site as a result. The domain name is like a map to your business: it needs to be a good signpost to how to get there.

If you're stuck, think about the words that most closely collocate with your site, and stick them into a thesaurus. Consider creating a mindmap, with the site's central position described in a couple of words in the middle of a large sheet of paper, branching out into word associations. Check whether potential names are memorable by slipping them into conversation with someone and asking which they remember a few minutes later.

Look through the URLs in dropped domain databases, which list those that have just switched from being registered to available. You can find these on databases like domainsuperstar.com and justdropped.com. Note you don't have to use these sites to buy the name.

The cost of buying a domain from another user or auction will range from a few pounds up to millions for the most popular domains. But to register a URL, a .co.uk address costs only around £3 a year (for a minimum of two years) whilst a .com or .biz address is about £10 a year.

If you want your company name and domain name to be the same, research and buy the domain before registering your business name at Companies House. Some URLs will be out of your price range – no point drumming up interest in a brand if it's going to be called something else later on. But don't obsess with having the names match up – it's not crucial. Nick Jenkins at Moonpig originally registered his company as Moonpig. But he later ended up changing its name at Companies House to 'Altergraphics Limited' to appease investors.

Is it available?

Use www.whois.com, which lists domain name registrations, or use web hosting firms like www.123-reg.co.uk or www.fasthosts. com to check if a site is available. If the name is taken, think about whether you want to contact the owner via the details on whois to offer to buy the site.

If it is available, register the domain as quickly as possible. Like seats on budget airlines, domains get more expensive once they start receiving more search traffic. Register a domain via one of the ISPs or domain name registrars listed on Nominet, the not-for-profit organisation that manages .co.uk registration (www.nominet.org.uk/registrants/register/ agent/). Shop around before picking one firm – they will each offer different fees, services and contracts.

Watch out for copyright issues: a domain name is intellectual property, so don't name your site anything like an existing brand or name. If in doubt, ask Nominet to carry out a thorough search.

Remember, too, to watch your domain expiration dates. They have to be renewed – usually once a year – so don't forget. If it becomes unregistered and someone else buys it, you'll either have to buy it back or will have wasted a lot of time and money on marketing.

Hosting

You can choose to either pay for storing, serving and maintaining files so visitors can view a site – known as website hosting

– or you can go down the free route. Hosting space is available free from the likes of BT (to home broadband customers) and Google, but will come with site advertisements. The speed and reliability may also not be as good as via a paid host. Free hosts also tend to impose a limit on the traffic a site can use per day and per month – so if you're expecting large volumes of traffic (bandwidth) or your site contains huge numbers of images or videos, it's best to opt for a commercial host. If you're building your site with open-source software, you can host on the Heroku platform (heroku.com) for free. It provides enough power for a few concurrent users, which can be plenty to test an idea before handing over more cash for full-scale hosting later on. You'll find plenty of developers happy to answer questions on the issue on Twitter – most will be eager to talk about the various options and their experience.

Commercial hosting will cost from £7 per month. You'll be given options of payment plans (monthly, quarterly, annual) – the former is usually best at first as you check whether you're happy with the reliability and speed. Compare the bandwidth, speed, technical support, disk space, and email provision offered by each package. Or opt for dedicated hosting, on an individual server. At a cost of more than £50 a month, you'll only need this if you are expecting large volumes of traffic, using huge amounts of images or videos, or if security is crucial for your site. Running on your own server will help you stay as close as possible to 100% uptime.

Build, design and development

With web host and domain name organised, it's time to design the site. Whether you're going down the DIY route or outsourcing, you'll need to work out a rough site design – what features do you want, how many pages and what will they contain, what colours or images will dominate. Create some different looks ready to be honed by a designer or translated into code by you or a developer. Decide whether you want to go down the lean route by creating a bare-bones prototype (wireframe) then honing the site as analytics and user feedback reveals what is missing or could be improved – or a 'big reveal', creating a site that's closer to its finished status when it goes live. Most developers, product managers and other online professionals now promote the former strategy: it's more fruitful to react to users' needs from the start. Otherwise, you're potentially wasting a large amount of time – and money – on a site that either doesn't work, or doesn't match users' needs.

No budget?

Then create your own site. There are hundreds of online templates available, often free, via sites like Moonfruit.com and Wordpress.com. Note, though, that these offer only limited scope for personalisation, and basic features. The next step up is a cheap DIY package from companies who offer combined web building, hosting and domain name deals. MrSite has a beginners' takeaway website pack for £24.99 a year. The basic site has five pages, five email addresses, one domain name, and 75 Mb of web hosting. Two more expensive packages provide more space, emails and an online shopping feature. Moonfruit offers similar deals. Or you could opt for a 'what you see is what you get' design software like Dreamweaver to create a site.

The designer/developer route

If you want something more high-tech, unless you're an IT genius or have one signed up as a co-founder, you're going to have to pay for it. Start your search for a web designer and developer – they're different skills but a good firm or individual will have access to both – by asking around. Entrepreneur networking groups are a good starting point, or browse sites you like and find out who designed them. Look at the company or designer's previous projects. Fees will range from £200 for a basic site with a few pages, to tens of thousands of pounds for a busy, complex site with serious backend functionality.

You'll need to give a developer a clear brief, and they should provide a number of different designs for you to select or hone before going on to create them. Make sure they choose a platform that other developers can work with – otherwise you'll be totally reliant on one developer, and could be held at ransom on fees. Industry standard platforms include Ruby on Rails, J2EE or Microsoft's .NET; whilst open source options include WordPress, Joomla and Drupal. Be cautious about allowing a developer to opt for a proprietary platform they own – or, if you do, at least ensure they have an open set of rules (known as an API) allowing third parties to work on it. The platform you opt for now will determine the pool of talent from which you can recruit later on, as developers need to be able to code in that language.

The top thing you should look out for in a developer is 'someone who asks more questions about your idea than you', according to Rob Cooper, a developer with experience working with big corporates, who has recently started his own venture, personal finance site Moflo.co.uk. This, he adds, will mean that developers want to (and will) understand your idea. 'Understanding the problem is key to developing the right solution', he adds. 'Ask them about products they have delivered in the past. What does it take to deliver that? Developers should also validate their work as early, and as often, as possible. Even better, ask the potential customer to validate the work to check usability. They should regularly drop pages to a UAT [user acceptance testing] environment, where ordinary online users test your site. Or if you are really brave, and have solid, reliable developers, they could even take the changes straight to live and start measuring and learning from the impact immediately.'

Speed-dating for developers

A website can always be changed, but only if you have a workable and productive business relationship, says Leigh Caldwell, online entrepreneur behind pricing software group Inon. Having spent almost two decades running a web development agency, here he reveals exactly what online entrepreneurs should ask of their developers.

1. Understanding

Make sure the developer understands how people will use the site, how they will think and feel about it – and that they can build it accordingly.

Key questions to ask yourself:

- What is your developer's understanding of the likely audience?
- What experience do they have working with that audience in the past, and on which types of application? Ask to see websites and speak with past clients.
- How will the site be tested with real consumers to make sure they behave how we want them to – in terms of spending time on the site, or buying products, or anything else important?

2. Changing the site

However good the design and backend of a website, something unexpected is guaranteed to happen as soon as you launch. And then again the next week, and four more times in the next few months. Your site has to be flexible enough to be changed quickly – within a few hours or at most a couple of days – in response. It could be a bug, or a legal issue like an error in the terms and conditions or a missing opt-out box, or a commercial opportunity like the chance to do a joint promotion with a new partner, or to respond to a topical news item and capture some instant PR. You need to be able to change the site quickly and inexpensively. Copy changes, price and product changes should be under your control, not the web developer's. Ideally, so should graphics, menus and other items.

Key questions to ask a developer:

- What ability will I have to edit the site myself? Does this include text, graphics, menu items, prices, tax rates, delivery fees, fields on input forms?

- What kind of changes do you anticipate making to the site after launch, and what would be the costs of doing so? Please provide examples of prices for individual changes, not just day rates.

- What is your approach to version control and rollback (of code changes and data updates)?

3. Responsiveness and reliability

Set particular standards for response times per page, or agree that a customer satisfaction standard will be applied. You can also agree downtime limits – which you should express in an average downtime per year rather than a percentage basis; 99.9% uptime sounds great, but it allows nine hours per year of downtime. It's easier to make the decision as a number of hours than a percentage.

Have a frank conversation with the developer about likely volumes – there is no point investing in a major scaling capabillty If you never expect to have more than ten customers a day. But if you want to allow for a million a day, design the site and its code accordingly.

Key questions to ask a developer:

- How many transactions, or customers, or what volume of data, will the site be able to cope with at launch? What will be needed to expand it for higher volumes (hardware, software licences, more development work)?
- What maximum amount of downtime will you commit to? How is downtime classified (e.g. if one feature of the site is down but the rest is running)?
- Who will provide hosting and on what terms?
- Is there a backup server in case of hardware problems with the first server? Will it switch over automatically?

4. How well does it support your marketing activities?

Discuss search engine optimisation strategies (see Chapter 17 on marketing) and landing pages – you should be able to create new ones as needed to support any marketing campaigns you might want to try.

Key questions:

- How will automated emails be handled? Can I edit them? How will they get through spam filters?
- What analytics or traffic logs will be provided?
- What reports will be provided?
- Whose responsibility is it to promote the site after launch? How will they work with the developers if any changes are needed?

5. Control

You need to be able to appoint additional developers or even walk away from your existing relationship if something goes wrong – so choose a platform that other developers can work with (see above). Ownership of the code developed for your site can be a sticky issue. Many developers have an existing library of tools that they have previously built, which they may want to use on your site. You don't necessarily need to own everything in your site. But you should insist that any code that you don't own has clear published documentation which enables others to use and modify it. If any licence fees are payable for this code, find out in advance what they are, and the implications for scaling up your website. Pay less for the project if it uses existing code as part of the build – try to get a comparative quote from a team which will let you own everything they create for you.

Key questions:

- What platform and software will be used? Who will own the resulting software?
- Are there published APIs for any proprietary products?
- What end-user documentation will be provided (for example, if your staff will be using a content management system or a wiki)?
- If there is any source code which we will not have access to, will you put it in escrow?

6. Flexibility

Whatever you think you're going to build today, within a few months things will have changed. Modern web technologies make it very easy to iteratively change your site and add new functionality. Make sure your commercial relationship reflects this. Ask for an estimate of overall project cost, then insist it's broken down into small chunks. If you plan a six-month project quoted at £100,000, break the contract up into 20–40 individual features, each of which can be delivered within a week or two, and agree a separate price for each one. Then, commit only to the first few, so that after each new incremental piece is delivered, you can re-evaluate and decide what you want to do next.

Key questions for your developer:

- Can you provide examples of fixed price changes on similar projects?
- Do you carry out continuous integration and incremental development?
- How many iterations should we expect on each feature?

7. You have to be important to your developer, but not too important

Try to find a developer that is big enough to support you, and who won't be under financial pressure if they overrun on their timetable and you hold up payment. But make sure they are small enough that you get senior management attention, and that they need to commit to making your project successful.

Key questions:

- How big is your company?
- What is your financial position (in general terms – they may not want to give specifics)?
- How many staff, and at what seniority, will be involved in our project? How much of their time will we get?
- How will the agreed payment terms ensure fair incentives on both sides to get things right?

8. Responsibility

Who will be responsible for bringing all the different aspects of a website (graphics, HTML layouts, CSS stylesheets, software code, existing data, payment processing systems, supply chain partners like a parcel delivery system, social networking sites, hosting, email servers) together? If you don't have the in-house skills, make one supplier responsible for integrating testing and delivering the work of all.

Key questions:

- What are the different responsibilities in the process and who is in charge of each?
- Who is responsible for paying third parties and under what terms?
- Who provides and populates test data? Who cleans it out after testing?
- Who is in charge of project planning?

9. A clear plan for the future

Delivering the site is one thing, and the day you go live is a time for celebration – but it will also need to be supported over time. First, bugs. Inevitably one or another will crop up. Your contract with the developer should cover this. The standard method is to cover all bugs under a warranty for a fixed period after delivery (three to twelve months is typical); and then move onto a paid support contract where the supplier agrees to fix bugs in return for a monthly fee.

The second source of changes is environmental. Maybe a new browser version is released, or a new privacy regulation is issued preventing websites from using cookies in the traditional way. Treat these as commercial issues so you can decide whether to spend the money updating your site to cope with, say, a new browser.

Key questions:

- Is a warranty provided; for what period; and does the warranty start on delivery, on going live, or at some other date?
- When a bug or support request comes up after launch, how quickly will the developer respond and when will a fix be available? During what hours, and in what time zones, will support be available?

Checklist of extra questions:

- Will the site have its own built-in search?
- If there is a financial aspect to the site, will there be built-in audit trails, accounting transactions and so on?
- Will passwords be automatically changed; how will people get password reminders?
- Are there third-party certification requirements, like the bank having to certify site security before taking credit card payments? How will that be handled?
- What browser versions/platforms (PC, mobile) will be supported at launch?
- Who will provide a privacy policy and/or terms and conditions for the site?
- Does the site need to be internationalised or support multiple languages?
- Is the developer, and/or the client, in compliance with the Data Protection Act? Do they need to be?

- What security requirements does the site have – are there admin users with multiple levels of access to data; will the site be encrypted with SSL; what firewalls or other protections do the servers have?

Outsourcing development overseas

When looking at the various options for contracting out website development, it's worth looking beyond these shores. It can be cheaper to outsource the work abroad. When Tom Harris launched FindaBabysitter.com, an online childcare search site offering 60,000 nannies, babysitters and childminders, all background-checked, he initially hired a London web development agency. He had raised £420,000 funding from angel investors and, he explains, 'with that secure, I thought it would as simple as just getting the site built, then spending a few grand here and there to add new functionality.' But Harris struggled to overcome two problems. 'First, agencies always try and own the intellectual property (IP) to the code and, if they don't, they tend to be less concerned about its quality and scalability', he explains. 'And, second, they work on multiple projects. You never get a tech team "eating and breathing" your business because they have other tasks and deadlines for other businesses.'

Looking for alternative options – but without the techy ability to build the site himself, Harris decided to outsource to a team working exclusively for him, overseas. 'I wanted to build an offshore team where I had complete control, 100% ownership of IP, and the ability to wash my hands of all hiring and firing, payroll, disciplinary, vacation and sick-day management', he explains.

Harris eventually opted to outsource the work to a tech team based in Bulgaria. 'It is somewhere I could fly to from Heathrow in a few hours to spend a couple of days with the team at little cost and hassle.' That was crucial during the build phase, when he flew out to eastern Europe every six weeks. 'That ruled out India and the Far East was not an option. After going through a vendor selection phase, I went with a company called Quickstart which offered exactly what I wanted. They had an office in Sofia, where I built my team.'

Harris decided to make the Bulgarian side of his business as heavily involved in every aspect of the business as his UK staff. 'Every morning the dashboard, which shows all of our key metrics, is distributed amongst the team. Everyone is encouraged to feedback, give ideas and comment on any aspect of that. Not including the outsourced team in key performance indicators like revenue and targets is a big mistake', he says. 'You want their buy-in like any other team member. You need to build their trust and you need to identify leaders you can rely on early.'

The platform went live in December 2010. 'Now we have a really dedicated group of guys working out of Sofia', says Harris. Findababysitter, which has now hit 100,000 members, hosts monthly team meetings over Skype so all employees can be involved. 'We encourage all Skype calls in the office to be headset-free, so everyone knows what each other is up to, and people can jump in on any conversation.' The start-up has also hired a customer services agent based in Delhi, outsourced through a company called Virtual Employee. 'He is young, keen and, because we involve him in what the business is doing, shows an entrepreneurial side where he inputs ideas and feedback from customers, which is vital.'

The other side of the story
Outsourcing isn't for everyone. It may be harder to retain control over your work, since contractors are likely to be

juggling several contracts, and your ideas could – perhaps even literally – get lost in translation. Amanda Zuydervelt used realms of outsourcers to found Stylebible, an online directory of reviews of spas, shops, hotels and more in cities around the world, in 2005. With a career background ranging from chalet girl to computing but still in her 20s, Zuydervelt started reading. 'I read autobiographies of people who'd done it for inspiration, web-based books to get my head around the technology and business books to grasp things like VAT and accounting', she said.

Zuydervelt had been building websites for small firms for a few years, but they were effectively online brochures. 'The most programming required was creating a form, but my idea was for a big project with a huge database.' So the entrepreneur signed up to freelancing websites that allow users to post a brief for web work for coders to bid for. 'I outsourced to expert programmers using vworker.com, having also looked at elance.com and freelancers.net', says Zuydervelt.

'Running a start-up with little or no funding is possible', she says. 'I spent £2000 on outsourcing the branding and design, and created the pages with a friend in-house, literally, at home, so that just cost me cooking him dinner whenever he came over', she explains. 'I paid the programmer £5000 for the code at the start – it's crucial to own your own code – and it has cost about £3000 since. Using coders in India and China brought the costs down massively – and in fact made the site an afford-able ambition.'

Lessons
Anyone outsourcing aspects of development should set out a guarantee of frequent updates on real-time status and progress

in a contract. Demand visibility on all your issue logs, and think about any potential commercial conflicts: if providing access to a site's dashboard metrics or other performance data, ensure a confidentiality clause. Equally, try to protect yourself against a developer being lured into creating a similar site for a competitor.

Design: usability

It's all very well to build a beautifully colour-coordinated or strongly branded site, but if it's tough for users to navigate, then they'll quickly click away. User experience – or UX – should be a crucial part of your product. As UXers put it: thinking about the user experience of your site means making sure that the people who come to your website don't have to think. Everything should be clear, obvious, intuitive, and even delightful. If your site involves e-commerce, for example, ensure customers can make orders quickly and easily. Navigation should be intuitive and security a priority. Here, Yael Levey – a user experience consultant who has worked with sites including Moo, JustGiving and Mind Candy and is now launching start-up dreambigly. com – gives her top tips:

- **What is your site about?** Your homepage is an incredibly important screen, yet often people neglect key pieces of information. It should always, unequivocally, tell your visitors what your site is called, its purpose, and what they can do here.

- **Guide your users.** If your website has several pages, or you will be taking your users through a multi-step process, make sure that they always know where they are, and how they can go back, or go to the homepage. Make sure that the title of the page is clear and visible, and consider creating a breadcrumb trail so your users know at all times at what stage in a process they are.

- **Clickable stuff should be obviously clickable.** Links should be clearly marked, buttons should look like you can click on them, rather than just looking like images. Utilise 'hover' states – when a user lingers over something that they can click, the button or link should change to indicate it is ready to be clicked.

- **Keep it concise.** However well-crafted and nuanced your writing style is, people will not read every word on your site. They will scan for the most important points. Emphasise the most important points and cut out all the fluff.

- **Make it clear what is important.** Since people don't read webpages, they scan, bear this in mind when designing the layout of your page. There should be a clear visual hierarchy of information – the stuff that you deem most important should look like the most important thing on the screen. So the button that you want everyone to click on should be prominent, and the title of the page should be in the largest lettering.

- **Don't get too crazy.** It's tempting to want your site to be like something nobody has ever seen before, and to come up with all sorts of different ideas about how it should look and behave. Balance being unique with being usable and intuitive. Website conventions are so popular because they are tried and tested. People understand how to interact with them and what they do.

- **Keep it consistent.** Consistency is key to making your users feel like your website is a cohesive whole and for them to feel at home. Examples of things to keep consistent are 'close' buttons on pop-up windows, which should always be in the same place, and headers and footers, which should be the same across the site. Phrases and words you use to describe your product should be the same through your website, and indeed throughout your entire customer service experience.

- **Show the site to users (or anyone).** The best way to make sure you are on the right track with the design and UX of your website is to show it to people at any stage in the process. It's never too early to get whatever you have in front of people. Don't ask leading questions like 'Do you like my website?' You want to know if they understand what it is they are looking at. Ask them to do the common tasks that will be occurring on your website. For example, if you have an e-store, ask them to try and buy something. Don't provide too much help, just observe and see what they expect out of your design. Ask them to think aloud as they perform tasks. This should provide valuable insight into what is working, what isn't, and why.

SEO

Carrying out SEO – or search engine optimisation – is crucial to get a site known online. Do it properly and it will boost site visibility by sending it to the top of search engine rankings. SEO relies on you having specific keywords, requiring the right 'meta data'– page descriptions and keyword tags – when you build the site.

Think about SEO from the start – it's much tougher to shape later on once you've committed to development or to a specific content management system. 'It's like laying down the foundations for your new house', says Lee Allen – director of search at Stickeyes, a search marketing agency which advises brands including Phones4U, Lovefilm, and hair brand GHD on online strategies. 'You want your site to be sturdy, robust and standards-compliant, but flexible enough to allow expansion in the future.

'It's crucial to carry out site architecture and URL hierarchy analysis, which determines how your site is laid out. So, say, with online fashion retail, top level categories might include men's, women's and children's, with sub-categories shoes, dresses and so on. It may be that you only offer women's clothing currently and are inclined to only use the relevant sub-categories but think about future expansion.' 'Future-proofing' a site ensures you won't have to restructure its architecture later on. 'And remember, this work should always be informed by your initial keyword research. Google AdWords is a great starting point which can help guide your development.'

Optimise all title tags, keywords and descriptions, and heading tags. 'These are key elements within each page's source code, helping search engines to understand the structure of a page', says Allen. 'It's key to include the relevant target keywords.' So a sample heading tag might read, '<h1>Women's Maxi Dresses</h1>' whilst a title tag could be '<title>Women's Maxi Dresses | Women's & Ladies Dresses | Brand Name</title>'. Canonical tags help lessen duplicate content, by telling Google which is the main version of a given page where duplicate versions exist. An example canonical tag might read: '<link rel="canonical"href="http://www.yourdomain.com/the-correct-url/" />'

Site content

The reason someone carries out a search is to receive the right content – and they want the content they click on to be relevant and of good quality. 'When developing a page you need to be asking yourself "why would a user land here?" and "what would they be looking for?"' says Allen. 'The key elements are quality content, optimising content for the relevant (and highly searched) keywords, and the right type of content – should it be printed copy, a video, an image, or a combination of these.'

Just because your site says it's an authority doesn't make it so. 'This is where off-site factors such as links play a role', adds Allen. 'The main mistake that companies make over and over is acquiring an incorrect balance of links, which results in an unnatural link profile.' This generally swings one way or the other. Says Allen: 'Possibility one is that the link profile has a distinct lack of keyword focus so search engines can't see that the site is relevant to the keywords which the brand wishes to rank for. Or, possibility two is that large proportions of your links contain the same target keyword – e.g. "dresses" rather than a balance of keywords and brand variations, which is more natural in an unengineered profile. Or possibility three: the sites on which the links are being acquired are quality i.e. they have large amounts of external links to other sites, obvious paid links, or a lack of quality links coming into their own site.'

Social networking is one good source of links, and register your site on online directories like Google Places, Yelp and Qype, which then link back to your website. If customers review your site on the directories, it provides user-generated, new content, which will build your site's trust rating as well as its profile. Free Tools like www.opensiteexplorer.org/ can help you under-stand your link profile and help you find link opportunities to grow your organic search traffic.

CHAPTER 16

GETTING YOUR SITE KNOWN: MARKETING

You might have built the world's best new website, but if nobody's using it, it's about as useful as an error 404 page. You need to get your website's name around – and fast. This chapter is all about organising a marketing strategy, with tips from some of the best PR gurus in the business.

Some web entrepreneurs create an astonishing publicity splash for free – remember Moo founder Richard Morross' success contacting 100 top tech bloggers? That was enough to give his business a powerful launch without any serious financial investment. Others pour a sizeable proportion of a site's revenues or staff time into building its name, with traditional or non-traditional marketing. Think of comparison site GoCompare's operatic TV and radio advert, for example, or the extensive effort Enternships founder Rajeeb Dey put into social networking.

It's true that the best sites will, on some level, sell themselves – but the internet is a busy place. When thousands of shoppers pour into Oxford Street on a busy weekend, the huge number of store options mean that even retailers with a stand-out USP – those selling the most fashionable shoes or cheapest T-shirts, for example – have devised a marketing plan to draw customers in. The same principle applies online.

Creating a plan

You should, by now, know exactly who your target market is, so the next step is working out the best way to attract them. Set up clear goals – what do you want your marketing to do: attract as many web-users as possible to your site, regardless of their interest or requirements? Direct only tennis-lovers to making a purchase in your Grand Slam e-store? Encourage existing site-users to sign up to your weekly newsletter? Whatever your objective, direct your publicity accordingly. Work out a budget and timetable – are you setting aside more time and cash for a big splash at launch, or having a soft opening with just a few Google Adwords directly promoting traffic? What timescale do you want to achieve your aim, and what will you do next? How will you measure your success – sales, customer contact details, website analytics, press coverage, or hits?

Don't chuck all your money at one strategy. If a potential customer sees a Tweet about your site re-tweeted by a friend, then reads about your online competition in a newspaper and then sees you, the founder, interviewed about life as a start-up on TV, they're far more likely to remember and use the site than if they'd just seen that single Tweet.

Write a list of every communications channel that's related to your market. Where are your potential customers finding out about the next big thing, or getting their information and entertainment? Is it word-of-mouth referrals, TV, Facebook, Twitter, directories, newspapers and magazines, online newsletters, Google, industry round-ups, trade papers, or somewhere else? These areas all need content – you can provide it for free, or advertise on it.

The theory

Desire is the most powerful asset in marketing, says Michael Hayman, co-founder of the entrepreneurs' communication consultancy Seven Hills who is also chairman of entrepreneurs at the bank Coutts. 'If you can get someone to want something, they will buy it. It's a simple truth that underpins the success of the most desirable brands in the world. It explains why, in sector after sector, companies now spend more on marketing than they do on R&D.

'The opportunities of the web are brilliant – an endlessly accessible street, with millions of shop windows, and countless numbers of consumers. You are never more than a mouse click away from a customer, so getting noticed is crucial. Technology means you don't have to spend a fortune to get your message across. But even if you aren't spending the money you are still dealing with your most valuable asset, your reputation. It is something you need to see in commercial terms, because if there is one lesson in business it is that cheap can be very expensive.'

So, how to stand out from the crowd? Don't, as the marketer Seth Godin puts it, 'taste like chicken'. Hayman explains: 'Bland is your enemy, brilliant is your goal.' His three 'D's' to help online businesses communicate brilliantly are:

- *Distil.* Language is a craft, not a commodity. In the battle for attention you need to make less count for a lot more.
- *Differentiate.* Make your bid for attention as different as you can. Be a challenger and disrupt the status quo.

People's minds are saturated by too much information about products and services that all look the same. In this environment, difference matters.

- *Discover.* Knowledge is power, so learn about your customers. Mark McCormack, the sports marketing agent and inspiration behind the movie character Jerry McGuire, put it like this: 'All things being equal people will buy from a friend, all things being unequal people will still buy from a friend.'

The reality

Five things will help drive traffic to your site: word-of-mouth recommendations, PR and networking in the real world, and SEO, pay-per-click advertising and social marketing online.

The first – referrals – should come naturally if your site is fulfilling a need, serving a niche audience or doing something better than it was previously done. SEO is important whilst building and developing a site, and is discussed in the previous chapter. But pay-per-click advertising, PR and social marketing are things you can choose to devote more or less of your time and budget on.

Pay-per-click

There's one big caveat to all that SEO work – there is one way to guarantee your place at the top of search results pages: buy your place. You can purchase search words and phrases that are relevant to your business – so a shoe etailer might buy 'cheap shoes' or 'high heels', for example. With PPC, you bid against other potential buyers to buy words. The search engine then decides where and when to place your ad, according to your bid, and you're charged a fee each time a web surfer clicks through to your website. The biggest players in the market are Google Adwords and Yahoo!'s Advertising.

Before you go down the PPC route, work out your conversion rate – on an online shop, for example, this would be number of visitors per month divided by number of sales per month; if your monetisation policy involves getting people to sign up to a newsletter, that figure would replace sales. Once you've worked out a cost per lead, set the budget to spend on a keyword accordingly. If your conversion rate is 5%, you'll be willing to spend more than if it's 0.5%.

Google's Keyword tool (https://adwords.google.co.uk/select/KeywordToolExternal) shows the most searched-for terms and will help you work out the best target keywords. Strike a balance between most popular and most specific, as the former will be much more expensive. Once you've paid for a PPC campaign, remember to update your ad and investment regularly to ensure the keywords are generating business. Set up a spending cap, too, to avoid blowing your whole budget.

PR

It's often thought to be expensive, but it doesn't have to be. PR can help generate links, business and interest in your site – and you can start by doing it yourself. Sara Tye, founder of redheadPR, has worked with hundreds of businesses and was formerly the personal PR manager to the late Body Shop founder Anita Roddick. Her top tips for PR on a shoe-string are:

1. Think about a launch idea that stretches all marketing channels and then sustain it from there. Don't miss this opportunity.

2. Communicate everything that is relevant about your business – it's an opportunity to talk.

3. List all the external and internal moments that are linked to your brand and organisation such as Christmas, Easter, awareness days, big news events – and exploit them.

4. Start a database of contacts, consumers, opinion formers and journalists and keep this growing and evolving – don't avoid this: you will regret it in two years' time.

5. Write plenty of collateral that you can use time and time again. Do so especially in your quiet times – then you'll be ready when a journalist comes calling on the busiest day of your year . . .

6. Keep in contact – do something all the time, no matter how small, as long as it's relevant. It will keep audiences engaged.

7. Spend time building relationships – be that by networking with other businesses and entrepreneurs or customers – the key is to keep the brand at the top of your mind.

8. Monitor the results of your work, be it looking at retweets on Twitter or Facebook comments. Make sure it's working.

9. Keep a record of everything you have done. You will need to use it again.

10. Enjoy it. This is one of the best parts of the job – increasing sales, acquiring customers and, in the end, gaining recognition and being successful.

Practical ideas

Get in contact with journalists in fields related to your online business. So, if you've set up a version of YouTube that special-ises in helping car-owners repair their cars without calling in a mechanic, make contact with motoring journalists. Reporters are always looking for interesting interviewees, new trends or insightful article angles. Don't bombard them with contact, but make it clear that you're happy to comment on relevant topics. Then provide full contact details and be available as much as possible.

Bloggers can be phenomenally influential. Moo.com's Richard Moross credits some of the tech world's most high-profile bloggers for helping to launch his business. Contact those who specialise in your industry before launch to get them onside. 'Forum posting is key, and email marketing is a good way to increase hits to the site, but watch out: perceived spam can affect the perception of the brand', says Tye. 'Use individual emails rather than round robins if the message is more targeted and the pipeline smaller. Most people will reply.'

Consider launching a competition with a prize – but make sure you supply something 'suitable and of value', says Tye. A new consumer-facing website, for example, could partner with an online newspaper or other related site to advertise a giveaway which can then provide you with a pool of details of interested potential users. Tye adds: 'Average redemption rates can be around 3000 replies – and a lot of sites will then supply you with the email addresses.'

Contact a few PR agencies to find out their rates and work out whether it would be good value to bring in the professionals. Remember that, as a founder, the time you put into PR could be used elsewhere and it's a lot easier to launch a website than re-launch it. Cheaper PR options include hiring a marketing student – they'll be very passionate but any mistakes could be expensive. The website Student Gems lists hundreds of relevant students (www.studentgems.com).

Psss . . . I know a great website . . .

Never underestimate the powerful PR that is word-of-mouth referral. If someone has a great experience on your website, they're likely to tell at least one person about it, and that personal recommendation will be far more likely to be influential than an ad or guerrilla marketing. For many consumer-facing businesses, particularly ecommerce, that may involve customer service. Doing it yourself at the start should ensure great service and will also put you in a position to secure vital feedback direct from users. 'In the early days I responded to each and every customer email or called them if possible during the day', says Tom Harris at findababysitter. 'I took my phone and laptop with me everywhere, and answered every email as quickly as possible – even if it was 3 a.m. on Christmas day or I was on holiday.'

Social marketing

'A social media "guru" tells you that you must "leverage influencers," seek out potential "brand evangelists" and do everything in your power to combat "brand detractors" and make them happy. You duly follow their advice (they are a guru after all) and end up with a Facebook page you don't know what to do with (hell, you don't even have any pictures to put on there), a Twitter account with a stream of status updates that may include such anecdotes as "Hello Twitter, I don't know what to do with you" and "nice cheese sandwich for lunch," a LinkedIn profile that actually looks pretty good, you've had a great career

– consider yourself patted on the back. All of this stuff is definitely going to do something for your business – because, well, a guru told you it would.'

That's Heather Healy, head of social media at SEO specialist Stickyeyes, warning start-ups about how not to do social networking. 'People too often sign up to social platforms, hearing the hype about the latest big brand to generate two million sales through Twitter (Hello @DellOutlet) and hope that by pushing out marketing messages, they can do the same too. You can, but you'll have to work a bit for it', she explains.

Here are Healy's top tips for social networking success:

- *Start with Facebook, Twitter and LinkedIn* as primary channels, and consider going on to Flickr, foursquare, YouTube and Google+ later on, once you have your feet under the table.

- *Identify who you want to talk to.* If you are trying to establish a reputation, use Twitter and LinkedIn to generate a strong online identity. If you want to talk to consumers, choose the platforms that consumers prefer, not the ones you use. That might be MySpace, tripadvisor, Facebook, Quora, moneysavingexpert or a plethora of other social networks where you may or may not be able to help shape the conversation.

- *Think before you speak.* No one likes the show off at the gym who brags about which car he's getting next: make sure you're not just shouting about how great you are. Those who listen, prove they listen by recognising others and their skills and then add real value to the conversation are winners.

- *Start listening to what people are saying about you,* your industry and your competitors. Set up a Google Alert:

www.google.com/alerts based on keywords. Monitor brands, industry chatter (e.g. 'social media marketing') and how people are discussing you across the web. This doesn't just mean Twitter; it includes the entire, user generated web. Anywhere that someone can post an opinion can be picked up using this simple tool and fed into an RSS reader. Feed it through to your email so that you actually look at it.

The exceptions to this rule are social networks such as Facebook that are guarded by privacy restrictions. For these networks, a little bit more effort is required to monitor what your competition is up to within their Facebook pages. Healy recommends TwentyFeet (www.twentyfeet.com) for keeping track of competitors' Facebook pages and their growth figures. Manually having a look at their day-to-day activity across social channels will give you some insight into what is working and what isn't.

Twitter is excellently geared up for listening. Set up an account, add a descriptive bio to let people know what you're tweeting about and upload an image and a background so that people will be able to tell who you are. Once you've done that, it's time to listen: follow your competitors, industry experts and people of interest.

Use Twitter's native search function – or the more advanced functions in Hootsuite – www.hootsuite.com – to track keywords and be alerted when keywords are mentioned.

- *Connect.* Once you've listened, you'll find that there are conversations you'd like to get involved in. Share your thoughts and engage in dialogue. Connect with those who will connect with you. Shamelessly trying to engage Britney Spears in regular dialogue isn't going to work.

And don't bother asking her to retweet your content; she won't.

- *Provide valuable content.* People want to read, view and watch interesting stuff. The more valuable, interactive and exciting the content, the more likely it is that people will share it. Be yourself and add value. As a starting point, try searching LinkedIn for questions you can answer with LinkedIn Answers. Influential people will often ask questions using the platform so demonstrate your expertise. Likewise, ask questions too and build connections. Or join flickr's 365 project and post a photo of yourself every day, let people see what you're up to; or create a panoramic Facebook photo sequence, check out these great examples: http://mashable.com/2010/12/14/new-Facebook-profile-hacks/.

Social marketing is marketing on a new channel, it's no different to how you present yourself at a conference or on your website. What's different is that you can really show your true personality and sell yourself based on your knowledge and how fantastic you are. Go show off (but make sure you flatter everyone else around you too).

Don't forget the real world . . .

With all the lure of Twitter et al, don't neglect planet earth. Every entrepreneur in this book has grabbed opportunities from their professional network – be that the number of a great developer, an angel investor, or indeed a marketing opportunity. When the techy community – and bloggers – get excited, that quickly feeds into the media and consumers. Seek out local networking groups – near Old Street's 'Silicon Roundabout' in

London, for example there's the Silicon Drinkabout event on Fridays to bring together like-minded tech start-up folk. MeetUp.com lists other networking events, as does TechHub. com. Most are also talked about on Twitter and Facebook, so stay engaged – but don't forget to leave your laptop every now and then.

Is it working? Analytics

In most industries, it's tricky to tell how your customers found out about your business without asking them. On the internet, it's easy. The world of website analytics makes it relatively effortless to measure the value of every penny you're spending on marketing. You can find basic analytical data from free tools like Google Analytics, or more advanced packages like Core Metrics, which allows you to understand better which channels contribute to other channels sales. Both provide info on how people entered your website, where they came from, and what they do when they are on it. It can seem overwhelming, but here are the first things you should be monitoring.

- *Referral tracking.* This shows you where traffic is coming from, like a search engine or marketing email, business directory, forum comments, affiliate sites, social network-ing, or direct traffic, where users type your domain name into their browser's address bar. This enables you to track down brand mentions – and if someone's saying good things about your business, you can track down testimoni-als. If it's critical, you can start to tackle the complaints.
- *Search monitoring.* This helps you to monitor the queries being entered into your site's search facility, revealing which parts are most in-demand, and how user interest is

changing. This can help you develop your start-up in the way customers want it to.

- *Technology use.* Tells you whether your traffic is mainly coming from computers or smartphones, and which browsers most surfers are using. Helps you tailor the site's design to your users' needs.

- *Bounce rate.* Shows how many users visit a page, then immediately leave without engaging with it. It can flag up a usability problem with a particular page or even an entire site.

So build a dashboard containing all these key metrics, plus cost per acquisition, conversion rates and cost per registration – whichever is most valid for your business. Analytics should be ignored at your peril.

Chapter 17

EXPANSION AND EXIT

To sell or not to sell? To gun for organic growth or seek out investment for rapid expansion? These are some of the dilemmas that successful online businesses will face at some point during their lifespan. 'Most people have a get-rich-quick mentality that can cloud the way they view their business', says Rupert Hunt at SpareRoom. 'Get rich slow is far more rewarding long term if you get it right. If the plan is simply to retire young and rich and spend your days on the golf course, then go for it – but the challenge for me was about creating something worthwhile and durable first and foremost.'

Whatever your overall objective, any entrepreneur who has taken on funding will certainly need to consider an ultimate exit. 'Any VC will be wary about a business that hasn't planned any kind of sale or bigger strategy', says Alan Wallace at Octopus Ventures. 'They will, one day, want to see how they'll be getting their investment – and more – back.'

It's worth considering your dream exit – whether it's a private sale to a rival or someone higher or lower in your industry food chain, an initial public offering, a merger, or a sale to a publically-listed firm – from the point of start-up. Working out who could buy your company, and why they would be interested, can help you to tailor the way you build and grow your site. You may want to expand your business all over the world independently, or you may want to build a niche food website that could one day be swallowed up by Marks & Spencer. Either way, since the exit point is the time when most entrepreneurs make their biggest return on the business, it's certainly worth considering your potential options and preparing in case of any approaches.

Think ahead – a year or even more before you're considering making an exit or starting major expansion, you'll need to begin making sure that the site is not too reliant on you, the founder, but has a management team that can run it semi-autonomously. Ensure all the development ideas that you've perhaps traditionally kept swirling around your head or locked away on your iPad are formally set out in the business so your team can work towards them. Instead of focusing on day-to-day decisions, start focusing on the wider strategy, such as business relationships, acquisitions, international markets or potential buyers. Work out who would make more money from the site than you, or where you could take it to make more money out of it yourself.

Whilst it can be tempting to always think about cutting costs in a bid to ease cash flow, it's crucial to take stock of expansion opportunities when they arise. Examine whether the climate is right to either grow your existing customer base or to adapt in response to changing consumer requirements, perhaps in terms of site design, usability or customer service. Be attentive to opportunities to buy out a competitor – particularly if you're doing better than them in a downturn – as well as the chance to branch into foreign markets, or move into a related industry.

If your site is a success, consider adapting it into other technologies, like mobile apps. 'Making a Rightmove mobile app was useful because it was a bit like creating the site all over again', says Hunt. 'Doing it ourselves rather than outsourcing it was been a great way to re-evaluate our services and assess how they fit into a different format.' But before making any expansion decisions, make sure you have the right resources available and carry out market and user research just as you did at the point of start-up. Factor in the benefits you may enjoy from economies of scale and exposure to new customers, but check that you'll be able to afford – both in terms of financial expense and manpower – the work involved.

Acquisition

If you receive a bid approach for your site, make sure you've talked to a range of companies or individuals about a deal to ensure you're getting the best possible offer. Having several interested parties will give you more bargaining power to push the price up. But what's it actually like to build up a successful website and then receive a bid approach? In 1997, Marc Worth and his brother Julian, created a trend forecasting company Worth Global Style Network (WGSN), which developed to become what *The Wall Street Journal* called the 'fashion industry bible'.

By the early noughties, he and his brother started to consider an exit; then, in October 2005, they sold the business, by which time it employed 172 staff and bought in a turnover of £15 million a year, to publishing giant Emap for £140 million. 'We started stepping back a couple of years before WGSN was sold', says Worth. 'We wanted to make ourselves "dispensable" and spent the last two years at the business making sure the best team was in place, our accounting and operational processes were running smoothly and we had a pipeline of new business. It was important to be able to show potential buyers that the business would operate well without us, so we recruited and trained a very solid management team who could demonstrate the skills and experience required to maintain the company's operations going forward.'

The two brothers worked out the figure they were chasing for a sale. 'Our valuation was based on a multiple of forward Ebitda [earnings before interest, tax, depreciation and amortisation] and Julian and I always had a figure of £60 million each as a good number to be able to never have to worry about money again.'

'Emap', says Worth, 'had been watching us for some time but were dragging their heels. It was only when a piece appeared in the *Sunday Times*' business section, learning that we were about to appoint advisors for a sale with a figure set at £150 million, that they called the next day and said they wanted exclusivity.'

The brothers agreed, with four conditions. 'First, that the price was £150 million – the minute they chipped at price we would walk away. Second, it had to be all cash, no shares. Third, that we would walk out the door the day we sold. And fourth, that they had eight weeks to close the deal.' Ultimately, that took 11 weeks, but the Worths got all their other conditions.

Used to the autonomy of being an entrepreneur, Worth made it clear at the beginning of negotiations with potential bidders that he and his brother would only be interested in doing a deal where they could exit immediately. 'In fact, we announced the sale to the business at 10 a.m. on a Friday morning and by 11.30 a.m., we'd cleared our desks and had left', he says. 'I think it has to be that way. Emap didn't want us around – they needed to stamp their own mark on the business. And I couldn't have stood by and watch them make decisions that I didn't agree with.'

Worth woke around 7 a.m. on the day of the sale, and later drove to the offices of legal giant Clifford Chance in the City. 'By the time I arrived the room was full. From our side was me and Julian, our finance director, and the other option holders, plus advisors. The meeting finally adjourned at 3.30 a.m. and was followed by plenty of back slapping and handshakes, before a trolley with champagne arrived.' Worth went home at 4.30 a.m. and spent an hour talking to his wife 'about how our lives had changed and how we would keep the children's feet on the ground.'

He met his brother for a cappuccino at a branch of Caffe Nero at 8.30 a.m., before going to their office in Edgware Road to give a speech to the staff. 'Then we returned to our office to clear our desks – we'd been careful not to take too much earlier as this might have alerted staff that something was happening. I loaded up a flight bag with my laptop and a few photographs, and took it to my car.'

One of the last things Worth did that day was to go shopping. 'I'd had my eye on a Cartier Pasha watch for some time and had promised it to myself once we'd done the deal. I left the office around midday and walked down to Selfridges. In less than five minutes I blew £15,000 – the first of several extravagancies. What felt so strange – and still does to this day – is that I could do something like that without it making a dent in the bank balance. I'd never had any desire to buy a yacht, a home abroad, or a private jet.'

Like many wannabe entrepreneurs, Worth says he had started his business 'just wanting to be in a position where I never had to worry about money again', and, as he puts it, the success of WGSN and its subsequent sale meant it was 'mission accomplished'. With a dose of good luck, and, far more importantly, hard work and great ideas, an entrepreneurial dream was fulfilled.

His success and that of all the other online entrepreneurs in this book is inspirational. Hopefully, their achievements have encouraged you to start up your own internet business. Whatever your aim for an online start-up, good luck at achieving your very own 'mission accomplished'.

RESOURCES

Featured websites

Dreambigly.com – lifelist website

Enternships.com – entrepreneurial internship recruitment

Findababysitter.com

Gocompare.com – insurance comparison site

Groupon.co.uk – group discount booking site

Inon.com – pricing software site

JustGiving.com – charity sponsorship site

Made.com – discounted designer furniture

Match.com – dating site

Moflo.co.uk – personal finance website

Moo.com – business card website

Moonpig.com – personalised greeting cards

ParkatmyHouse.com – parking space website

Spareroom.co.uk – lettings website

WGSN.com – trends website

Wonga.com – internet money-lender

Zoopla.co.uk – property valuations and listings

Check it out

Survey Monkey – an easy way to make market research surveys surveymonkey.com

Networking

The National Federation of Enterprise Agencies: a network of local agencies committed to working for small and growing businesses www.nfea.com

The Federation of Small Businesses promotes and protects SMEs and start-ups www.fsb.org.uk

British Library Business & IP Centre (www.bl.uk) – runs workshops and networking events for entrepreneurs

Everywoman – female entrepreneur networking group http://www.everywoman.com/

Shell Livewire – for entrepreneurs aged 16 to 30 http://www.shell-livewire.org/

Open Coffee Club Meetups (http://www.meetup.com/opencoffee/)

London – Silicon Drinkabout event on Fridays

MeetUp.com lists networking events, as does TechHub .com.

Funding and banking

Angel investment matchmaking services – Angel Investment Network: angelinvestmentnetwork.co.uk and Venture Giant: venturegiant.com

Aspire – government-funded investment for women-run businesses: http://tinyurl.com/aspirefund

British Chambers of Commerce – www.britishchambers.org.uk for business news and networking help

Business Debtline – provides practical advice designed to help business manage financial difficulties – www.bdl.org.uk

Business Link: a huge government-funded resource with free guides to every aspect of starting a business: businesslink.gov.uk

Business Link's rates calculator – http://tinyurl.com/bizlinkcalculator

Community Development Finance Initiative – provide loans and support to businesses in particular areas: cdfa.org.uk.

Companies House – search company information and accounts and find out more about starting a business: Companieshouse.gov.uk

Enterprise Capital Funds – government-backed initiative can yield investments of up to £2 million on a matched funding basis: capitalforenterprise.gov.uk.

HMRC.gov.uk – the taxman

Nesta – a government source of business funding: nesta.org.uk/investments/portfolio

PKF – accountancy firm quoted in this book – pkf.co.uk

Registry Trust – check if a customer has any County Court Judgments awarded against them in England and Wales for non-payment of a debt: registry-trust.org.uk

Tax administration help – http://tinyurl.com/bizlinktax

Creating a website

Domain databases – domainsuperstar.com; justdropped.com

Domain availability – whois.com; 123-reg.co.uk; fasthosts. com

Nominet, the not-for-profit organisation that manages. co.uk registration – nominet.org.uk

Free online website templates – Moonfruit.com; Wordpress. com; MrSite.com

Intellectual Property Office (free IP Healthcheck tool) – ipo. gov.uk.

Marketing

Social networking: Twitter.com; Facebook.com; LinkedIn. com; FourSquare.com; Plus.google.com

Twentyfeet.com – for keeping track of competitors' Facebook pages and growth figures.

google.com/alerts – keep track of what people are saying about your business

SEO: Stickyeyes.com; screamingfrog.co.uk/seo-spider; google.com/webmasters/tools; opensiteexplorer.org; seomoz. org; seobook.com

Analytics – Google's Keyword tool – adwords.google.co.uk/ select/KeywordToolExternal

Core Metrics – coremetrics.com

PRs in this book: Seven Hills PR – wearesevenhills.com; RedheadPR – redheadPR.co.uk

More advice

Smarta.com

Realbusiness.co.uk

UKWDA.org

Startups.co.uk